An Introduction to Lloyd's

LLOYD'S
LLOYD'S OF LONDON

ISBN 1 870043 05 7

Typesetting, page layout and editorial services by the Distance Learning Division of the Chartered Insurance Institute, Sevenoaks, Kent
Production services by Book Production Consultants, Cambridge
Printed and bound by Butler and Tanner, Frome, Somerset

CONTENTS

1
INSURANCE

2
REINSURANCE

3
CLASSES OF BUSINESS AT LLOYD'S

4
LEGAL PRINCIPLES

5
AGENCY; LLOYD'S BROKERS

CONTENTS

CONTENTS

10

PREMIUMS AND CLAIMS PAYMENTS

INTRODUCTION

This study course has been prepared both to assist candidates studying for the Lloyd's Introductory Test and to inform anyone who requires a basic introduction to Lloyd's of London.

The course book covers the areas of study listed in the Lloyd's Introductory Test syllabus (reproduced hereafter).

The course book is by no means exhaustive and, since it has been prepared by individual contributors, it is not intended to be an authoritative statement. In consequence, Lloyd's Training Centre shall not be under any liability of any kind in respect of the contents of this course, or the reliance of any person thereon.

This study course replaces an earlier open learning package and consists of extensively revised material in reflection of the recent changes in Lloyd's market practice and governance.

The Lloyd's Training Centre thanks those in the Lloyd's community who have assisted in its production. The course has been edited by Colin Hudson, Insurance Education Services Officer.

At the end of each chapter, a glossary of terms contained within the chapter has been included as an aid to study. Within the text, the symbol ◆ is positioned either side of the term included in the glossary. The multiple choice questions and answers, at the conclusion of each chapter, have been taken from past papers for the Lloyd's Introductory Test. A self-test question paper, consisting of twenty questions from past tests, has also been included as a guide and aid to students preparing for the Lloyd's Introductory Test.

Lloyd's Training Centre,
London, January 1993.

LLOYD'S INTRODUCTORY TEST SYLLABUS

Purpose

To ensure that the new users of the Room have an understanding of the principles and practice of insurance, particularly as it relates to the business of the Lloyd's market, with particular reference to the roles of the brokers and the underwriters and their respective responsibilities.

Candidates will be required to reach a satisfactory standard in a test which will seek to establish that the candidates have an adequate knowledge of the following topics:

(A) **The basic purpose and nature of insurance and its value to the community**

(B) **Legal principles governing insurance transactions**

    (i)   utmost good faith and its significance in the relationship between underwriters and brokers;

    (ii)   basic essential principles underlying every contract of insurance, including the purpose and effect of warranties;

    (iii)   the duties and responsibilities of a broker and the simple basis of the law of agency.

(C) **The structure of the Lloyd's market**

    (i)   the nature of Lloyd's, that is a society of individual members operating in a market place and regulated by a Council;

    (ii)   the members of Lloyd's; their unlimited liability;

    (iii)   the grouping of members in syndicates and the basic role of underwriting agents;

    (iv)   the position of Lloyd's brokers in relation to the Society;

    (v)   the role and responsibility of an appointed underwriter of a syndicate;

    (vi)   market associations.

(D)   Lloyd's market practice

(i)   the method of conducting business in the Room, including brokers' and syndicate numbers and pseudonyms;

(ii)   the way in which a policy is prepared and processed;

(iii)   the role and responsibility of brokers in the handling of premiums;

(iv)   the role and responsibilities of brokers in the settlement and payment of claims;

(v)   the role and responsibilities of underwriting staff and the system of delegation and responsibilities within an underwriting organisation;

(vi)   the nature and importance of market agreements;

(vii)   the particular responsibilities of leading underwriters within the Lloyd's system, including the operation of leading underwriters' clauses;

(viii) the importance of prompt and efficient transfer of premiums and payment of claims;

(ix)   the importance of prompt and efficient handling of claims.

All questions shall be based on English law and practice.

Candidates will not be required to have a knowledge of changes in legislation, including statutory instruments issued under existing Acts, or insurance practice where changes occur less than two months prior to the test dates.

1

INSURANCE

A   How insurance operates

B   The functions of insurance

C   The limits of insurance

D   Insurance premiums

LEARNING OBJECTIVES

After studying this chapter, you should be able to:

▷ state the primary and secondary functions of insurance;

▷ explain the basic purpose and nature of insurance;

▷ identify and distinguish between insurable risks and uninsurable risks;

▷ discuss the methods of premium calculation.

INTRODUCTION

Life does not always 'go smoothly' for people. However much care we may take to avoid problems or to safeguard our goods (whether as private individuals or as companies), we can never be certain that we will be successful. If a problem occurs it could be expensive in terms of human suffering and/or financial loss.

However, people want to own houses, drive cars, fly planes and sail in boats without having to worry about the potential financial problems involved. Insurance exists to provide people with security; it is a means of helping the unfortunate few who suffer loss or who are involved in an accident. As early as the twelfth century there is evidence of insurance being transacted by merchants in northern Italy; it was their descendents who introduced marine insurance to Britain in the fourteenth century.

♦**Insurance**♦ is a device for handling some of the risks which individuals or firms run in connection with their daily lives or business activities. Hence, there are business risks and personal risks. Business risks include ♦**losses**♦ by fire, theft or by incurring liability at law. Every individual faces personal risks as their property may be destroyed or they may incur liability at law through careless acts. Personal risks are a relatively small, but vital, part of the business of Lloyd's (and of the insurance industry as a whole).

In this chapter we will look at the role of insurance in attempting to combat some of the problems created by risk. We will examine the functions of insurance, both primary and secondary, and we will consider insurance as a risk transfer mechanism. We will examine the benefits of insurance to the individual, to industry and to the country as a whole.

A

HOW INSURANCE OPERATES

Insurance exists to cover the financial consequences of events, which are undesired by the insured person or organisation, due to a fortuity which we can refer to as ♦**risk**♦.

Insurers do not cover speculative risks where there is a possibility of financial gain. Insurable risks have the characteristics of the insured being in a 'loss or no loss' situation. Certain other risks are uninsurable or insurers choose not to insure these risks: we will discuss this further in section C1.

Insurance provides financial compensation for the effects of misfortune. Funds to provide this financial compensation for the insured are built up by the insurers from the premiums paid by the persons or organisations purchasing insurance cover.

For each and every premium paid into these funds, the insurer accepts the risk of a considerably larger claim being made against his funds, should misfortune strike the policyholder.

Figure 1.1: Provision for claims

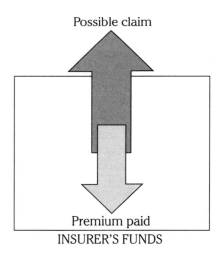

Possible claim

Premium paid

INSURER'S FUNDS

Insurance is thus a **risk transfer mechanism** and the insurers are the 'risk takers' in the final analysis.

Each policyholder should make a fair contribution to insurers' funds based on the degree of hazard associated with the risk and the values or liabilities at risk.

B

THE FUNCTIONS OF INSURANCE

Let us start by looking at the main functions of insurance before moving on to examine the benefits which can be derived from performing these functions. What is the role of insurance? What function does it perform? Let us answer these questions by considering the primary and secondary functions of insurance.

B1 PRIMARY FUNCTIONS

There are two primary functions of insurance, namely:

▶ to spread losses among many policyholders which would otherwise have to be met by individuals or individual firms;

▶ to reduce worry for the insured, by providing the security represented by insurance cover.

B1A Spreading of losses

The financial losses of the insureds are spread amongst all those who insure by compensating the few who suffer loss from the funds built up from the contributions of the many policyholders.

The spread of losses is equitable as each policyholder pays an amount commensurate with the risk introduced. Thus the contributions are not random or equal.

The function of the underwriter is the management of the fund and the assessment of equitable premiums.

Figure 1.2: Spreading of losses

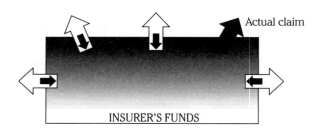

Actual claim

INSURER'S FUNDS

B1B Providing security

Whenever potential legal liability is involved, security is important; for instance, if motorists are not insured then they may have to pay out heavy compensation for another person's injuries, if they were held responsible. Likewise, a business protected from insurable losses will encourage business confidence.

In summary, insurance does not remove the risk; a house or factory may still burn down and a car may still crash causing personal injuries. However, insurance does spread the losses of the individual amongst the many policyholders, so that no one individual (or company) need suffer a heavy loss. Insurance reduces worry for the insured by providing security. It gives peace of mind and relieves policyholders from a great deal of potential financial hardship.

B2 SECONDARY FUNCTIONS

The secondary functions of insurance include the following:

▶ **Industries avoid the need to maintain funds to cover possible losses.** Instead they can pay a fixed contribution by way of premium and obtain financial security against the insured risks. Capital is thus freed for the further development of the business.

▶ **Security is provided to allow for the finance of overseas trade and the granting of mortgages.** Banks and other financial organisations require the security of marine insurance in financing home and overseas trade. Fire insurance makes it possible for property to change hands and for mortgages to be granted without fear of loss by fire and other perils.

▶ **The investment by insurers of their funds provides capital to industry and commerce.** Insurers are the custodians of the policyholders' premium funds and they invest these to earn interest.

▶ **Surveys and underwriting advice by insurers assist in prevention of loss, injury and fire waste.** Insurers place their knowledge and experience at the disposal of their policyholders. Insurers' rating methods also encourage minimisation of risk.

▶ **A substantial contribution is made to invisible exports through overseas premiums.**

Figure 1.3: Secondary functions of insurance

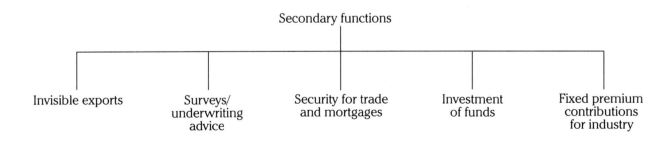

B3 BENEFITS TO THE COMMUNITY

In this chapter we have already dealt with many of the benefits of insurance to the community, i.e. security, risk transfer, loss prevention, investment in industry and invisible exports. Let us now consider the position if insurance did not exist and speculate who would compensate the injured motorist, for instance, or the persons who suffer damage to their property by storm. In many cases the task might well fall on the State and be passed to the community at large through taxation. As we have seen, the alternative is that the insurance funds built up by insurers are utilised for this purpose, thus indirectly benefiting the community as a whole.

THE LIMITS OF INSURANCE

Insurable risks must be fortuitous as far as the insured is concerned; be capable of being measured in monetary terms; and the insured must have a financial interest in the loss (termed insurable interest, which will be considered in chapter 4 under legal principles).

As time has gone on, man has devised ingenious ways of reducing the risk inherent in ventures of all kinds and new types of insurance cover continually are being developed. However, at present we can say that certain risks still remain outside the scope of insurance.

C1 RISKS NOT INSURED

There are various risks that are either not insurable or which insurers normally choose not to insure.

These may be defined as those risks which are contrary to the public interest, whether or not a specific exclusion is embodied in legislation; risks where the would-be insured has no insurable interest in the subject matter; and war risks other than certain specific classes where the accumulation of values is considered manageable in relation to insurance funds. For example, war risks cover may be given on ships, their cargoes, aircraft and on persons, but motor vehicles on land are excluded.

Risks arising through loss of market and economic conditions are not predictable and could be within the control of the person wishing to insure.

C2 INSURABLE RISKS AT LLOYD'S

Some risks (long-term life, for example) are not accepted because the Lloyd's method of individual underwriting is not equipped to handle them. Other risks are so speculative that they are uninsurable.

However, when a genuine interest exists and the would-be insured can show that he would suffer financially if the event insured against were to occur, then the risk usually can be covered at Lloyd's. For example, where the death of a judge hearing a lengthy civil case would result in a retrial with all its attendant expense, the litigants could insure his life to cover themselves against this contingency.

Lloyd's underwriters are known throughout the world for their willingness to insure unusual risks and for their flexibility. Risks of every conceivable description are accepted by underwriters from most countries either directly or by way of reinsurance (which will be considered in chapter 2).

Figure 1.4: Insurable risks at Lloyd's

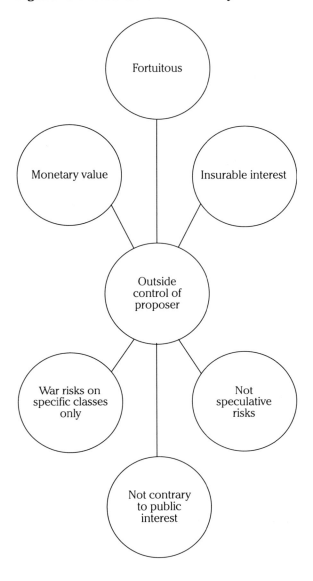

D

INSURANCE PREMIUMS

Q How is the cost of insurance calculated?

A The ◆**premium**◆ will relate to the amount to be insured (sum insured/limit of liability) and to the nature of the risk being borne by the insurer (frequency and severity of loss).

It is important to note that the contribution made by the insureds to this common pool (the premiums) will not be all the same.

Insurance is a risk-business: losses as well as profits can be made. Thus the insurer will minimise the possibility of losses by adjusting the premiums and terms of insurance according to the individual risks being brought into the pool.

Different members of the pool present different levels of risk to the pool itself. Thus there has to be some relationship between the likelihood of someone taking something out of the pool, and the amount they should put in.

D1 CALCULATION OF PREMIUMS

Premiums are normally arrived at by applying a premium rate to a premium base. The rate could be a rate per cent or per mille, applied to a figure which is the premium base. The rate is intended to reflect the hazard associated with the particular insured and the premium base is the measure of the exposure.

For example, an oil refinery valued at millions of pounds would cost more to insure than a private house valued at thousands of pounds. The sum to be insured for the oil refinery quite clearly would be greater.

Also, an oil refinery in certain parts of the Middle East with a long history of political unrest and armed conflict would cost a great deal more to insure than a similar oil refinery in Hampshire. The potential risk to the insurer would be greater.

When calculating the premium, it is important to note that both the insurer and the proposer contribute something to the calculation. The proposer defines the sum insured (value of the risk) and the insurer sets the rate to charge on that risk.

This is calculated as follows:

Premium = sum insured x rate per cent

The ◆**rate per cent**◆ is a figure set by the insurer based on the likelihood that he may have to pay a claim on the policy. Therefore the greater the risk to the insurer, the higher the rate per cent, and vice versa. A rate per cent is the amount in pounds charged for each hundred pounds of risk insured. For example, a rate per cent of 1.5 would mean that an insurer would charge £1.50 premium for every £100 of risk insured.

The term ♦ **rate per mille** ♦ simply means that the rate is quoted as so many pounds per thousand pounds insured.

While the sum insured is a suitable premium base for many property insurances, it would not be appropriate for liability insurance. In the case of employers' liability, the wage roll of the insured is normally used. Public liability is often rated on turnover and professional indemnity is rated on fees earned.

'H/c ?

Minimum premiums may be charged in some cases, such as with household contents, to reflect the cost of acceptance of the business.

Motor insurance premiums are based on the grouping of the vehicle with additions for excess value. Discounts are allowed for claims-free driving, voluntary excesses and restricted driving.

Life premiums are based on mortality tables (which show the number of people in a group who will survive for a given number of years), with allowances for expenses and reserves for unexpected contingencies.

D1A Calculation of rate per cent

Taking property insurance as an example, the rate per cent is calculated from statistics which have been collected over many years and which detail the amount of claims actually paid out over a given period (losses) compared with the total amount that could have been lost over that same given period, if every policyholder had made a claim (values-at-risk). The formula used is to multiply by 100 the ratio of losses to values at risk:

$$\frac{\textbf{Losses}\text{ (actual claims made)}}{\textbf{Values-at-risk}\text{ (total claims possible)}} \times \frac{\textbf{100}}{1} = \textbf{Rate per cent}$$

Let us now work through an example:

If £450 million worth of property values insured give rise to £9 million in actual claims, then the rate per cent for future premiums on this type of property insurance would be worked out as follows:

$$\frac{£9,000,000}{£450,000,000} \quad \text{x} \quad \frac{100}{1} = \text{Rate per cent}$$

This simplifies to:

$$\frac{£9}{£450} \quad \text{x} \quad \frac{100}{1} = \text{Rate per cent}$$

which is:

$$\frac{£900}{£450} = 2\%$$

Thus the rate per cent is 2%.

In general, the premium must be sufficient to cover expected claims. The law of large numbers allows the underwriter to make a reasonably accurate assessment of the likely claims costs and, at the very minimum, the premium must be sufficient to meet these expected claims.

D1B Additions to rate per cent

Added to the rate per cent calculated in this way is an additional percentage which is to cover items such as expenses (including commissions), profit and an estimate for outstanding liabilities.

Outstanding liabilities
Not all claims will be settled during the year for which the premium has been paid. This has been particularly true in the case of claims involving personal injury and legal liabilities, as these often take several years to settle and the underwriter must take this into account when calculating the premium.

Syndicate expenses
The insurer has a number of operational expenses to meet in the running of the business which, in the case of Lloyd's syndicates, include:

▶ salaries to staff;
▶ premises costs;
▶ brokerage;
▶ Corporation of Lloyd's expenses. *└ complaints only*

Provision for profit

The underwriter must ensure that there is provision for a reasonable <u>profit</u>. Underwriting members of Lloyd's expect a return on their membership of a syndicate. *used to*

The underwriter must consider some other factors in calculating the premium. These will include the following:

▶ the fact that the premium is paid now for losses which may arise in the future;

▶ possible changing exchange rates for an underwriter who accounts in sterling; and

▶ the effect of competition where charging too high a premium could result in loss of business but charging too low a premium could contribute to the syndicate running at a loss.

D1C Gross and net premiums

The insurer then uses his determined rate per cent to calculate the ◆**gross premium**◆ to be charged to the insured. The gross premium includes the amount of money paid to the broker for bringing this particular piece of business to the insurer. This amount of money is called the ◆**brokerage**◆ and usually is quoted as a percentage of the gross premium. For example, we might say in a particular case that the brokerage is 20%. We mean that the broker will be paid 20% of the gross premium and the insurer will take the remaining 80%. The amount of the premium left after removing the brokerage and any other deductions is called the ◆**net premium**◆.

To simplify this we can say that:

Net premium =gross premium minus brokerage

Q The hull value on a small pleasure boat is £2,000. The insurer sets a rate per cent of 10% and agrees a brokerage of 20%. What is the net premium?

A
Gross premium	= sum insured x rate per cent
	= £2,000 x 10%
	= £200

Brokerage	= 20% of gross premium
	= 20% of £200
	= £40

Net premium	= gross premium - brokerage
	= £200 – £40
	= £160

D1D Adjustable premiums

In some cases the final premium will not be known at the commencement of the contract of insurance. This applies to employers' liability risks, for example, where the premium is based on the estimated wage roll and adjusted on the known final figure at expiry. Some public liability risks are also subject to adjustment.

Similarly, money insurance is adjusted on the basis of the actual aggregate amount of money in transit during the policy period.

D1E Return of premiums

Partial returns of premium may be allowed under cancellation conditions in some policies. Under motor and home insurance policies, for example, if underwriters cancel the insurance then they return a pro rata premium. However, if the insured cancels then the return is based on short period rates to cover expenses of the underwriter.

Marine hull policies also contain provision for return of premium if the policy is cancelled by agreement and in certain cases when the vessel is 'laid-up' in port.

SUMMARY

We have dealt with a number of important features in this chapter, including the functions of insurance and the benefits to the individual person or company and to the economy. We have also considered the calculation of insurance premiums.

The insurer may also try to minimise any loss by insuring some of his commitment. This insurance by the original insurer is known as **reinsurance**, a concept which we will discuss in the following chapter.

1
GLOSSARY OF TERMS

Brokerage
The commission received by a broker for placing insurance risks on behalf of the insured. In practice it is paid to the broker by the underwriter out of the gross premium. However, the expression also means the business of the broker.

Gross premium
The full amount of premium, ignoring taxes or deductions.

Insurance
A means whereby the losses of the few are distributed over the many.

Loss
A claim under a policy. The financial loss caused to the insured by the happening of the event insured against.

Net premium
The amount of the premium left after removing the brokerage and any other deductions.

Premium
The amount paid to an insurer or reinsurer in consideration of his acceptance of a risk.

Rate per cent
The price in pounds for each hundred pounds of insurance.

Rate per mille
The price in pounds for each thousand pounds of insurance.

Risk
A fortuity; it does not embrace inevitable loss. The term is used to define causes of loss covered by a policy.

1

MULTIPLE CHOICE QUESTIONS

1. A slip contains the information that the value of an insured risk is £360,000. The premium rate is 1.25 per mille and the total discounts (including brokerage) amount to 20%.

   What net premium will the insurer receive?

   (a) £4,500.
   (b) £3,600.
   (c) £450.
   (d) £360.

2. A dress designer wants to insure against his new line of clothes not being a success. Why would he not be able to arrange cover?

   (a) Because the risk is a trading risk.
   (b) Because there would not be a financial interest in the subject matter.
   (c) Because the risk is too speculative.
   (d) Because there is no insurance market for clothing risks.

3. Which term defines 'peril'?

   (a) The estimated probability of a loss.
   (b) A fortuitous event which may cause a loss.
   (c) A condition which would increase the probability of a loss.
   (d) The total value of a possible loss.

4. The premium rate is 5% on a hull value of £2,000,000. Brokerage is 20%. The net premium is:

   (a) £120,000;
   (b) £100,000;
   (c) £80,000;
   (d) £20,000.

1

MULTIPLE CHOICE QUESTIONS

5. Which one of the following classes of business **cannot** normally be underwritten at Lloyd's?

    (a) Loss of aircrew licence.
    (b) Short-term life.
    (c) Financial guarantee.
    (d) Surety.

6. Which one of the following would be classed only as a secondary function of insurance as distinct from a primary function?

    (a) The provision of financial compensation for the effects of misfortune.
    (b) Surveys by insurers to assist in preventing losses.
    (c) A risk transfer mechanism.
    (d) The spreading of losses of the few amongst many policyholders.

ANSWERS TO MULTIPLE CHOICE QUESTIONS APPEAR OVERLEAF

1
ANSWERS TO MULTIPLE CHOICE QUESTIONS

1. Answer (d), £360:

Gross premium	=	£360,000 x 0.00125 (or 0.125%)
	=	£450

Discounts	=	£450 x 20%
	=	£90

Net premium	=	£450 – £90
	=	£360

2. Answer (a), because the risk is a trading risk.

3. Answer (b), a fortuitous event which may cause a loss.

4. Answer (c), £80,000:

£2,000,000 x 5%	=	£100,000 (gross premium)
£100,000 x 20%	=	£20,000 (brokerage)
£100,000 - £20,000	=	£80,000 (net premium).

5. Answer (c), financial guarantee.

6. Answer (b), surveys by insurers to assist in preventing losses.

2

REINSURANCE

A Reasons for reinsurance

B Main methods of reinsurance

C Reinsurance premiums

LEARNING OBJECTIVES

After studying this chapter, you should be able to:

▷ explain why insurers seek reinsurance;

▷ identify the main methods of reinsurance, both proportional and non-proportional;

▷ calculate the amounts ceded to reinsurers under various classes of treaty;

▷ identify and explain the main terms used in connection with reinsurance transactions.

INTRODUCTION

In chapter 1 we noted that one of the essential features for a risk to be insurable was the need for the insured to have an 'insurable interest' in it. Since Lloyd's underwriters accept risks, via the broker, from the public, they also meet this criterion.

The underwriter tries to ensure that a reasonable profit is returned to underwriting members from carrying the risk. Having accepted a risk the underwriter is really in much the same position as the insured in relation to the various uncertainties associated with the risk. Will there be a loss or not? If there is a loss, how large will it be? The insured was faced with these problems and chose to pass the risks over to the underwriter (we referred to insurance as a risk transfer mechanism).

Underwriters, despite their underwriting skills, are not immune to the possibility of larger than expected losses or more losses than anticipated. They have to charge a premium at the start of the insurance year for losses which will arise in the future. Thus looking at the insurer's risk, it is not surprising that they, in turn, seek insurance protection. The insurers insure the risk again, which is called ◆**reinsurance**◆.

As with the insurance market, the reinsurance market involves dealings between those who provide insurance (the sellers), those who wish to be insured (the buyers), and intermediaries (brokers). However, the difference is that in the reinsurance market the buyer (the underwriter) almost certainly will be well informed about reinsurance. Reinsurers themselves will want to spread some of their risks still further and so will be both buyers and sellers: this is termed a ◆**retrocession**◆. Lloyd's underwriters both reinsure their own risks and accept reinsurance from others through brokers.

Reinsurance is basically an extension of the concept of insurance, in that it passes on part of the risk for which the original insurer is liable.

A contract of reinsurance is between the insurer and reinsurer only and legally there is no direct link between the original insured and any reinsurer.

Figure 2.1: Reinsurance

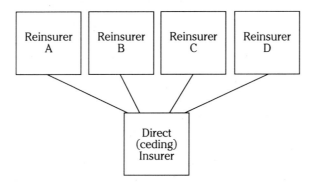

(The proportions reinsured may not be equal, nor may more than one reinsurer be involved.)

A

REASONS FOR REINSURANCE

? Why should insurers buy reinsurance?

We have answered this question to some extent in the introduction to this section, but there is more that can be said. The reasons could be itemised as follows:

▶ **Protection or cover against exceptionally large individual losses.** Let us consider two examples:

Example one
A fire occurs in an oil refinery which has an insured value of £120 million. The total material damage losses are £20 million. An insurer has

agreed to take 10% of the risk, thus he is liable for a loss of £2 million. The insurer may be able to recover part of this loss from a reinsurer if he has made suitable reinsurance arrangements. Thus he is protected from a large loss arising on one policy.

Example two
An insurer receives claims under 20 separate policies covering various insured premises in a large city hit by an earthquake. The total cost of this disaster to reinsurers is £120 million and the total of the claims on the one insurer is £4 million. Adequate reinsurance arrangements (catastrophe excess of loss) would protect him from an accumulation of losses arising from a number of policies.

▶ **Avoiding undue fluctuation in underwriting results.** The aim is to secure a balanced account and results each year without 'peaks and troughs'.

▶ **To obtain an international spread of risk.** This is important when a country is vulnerable to natural disasters and an insurer is heavily committed in that country but perhaps not writing direct risks in others which do not have the same problems.

Example
An insurer writes a large account in the Caribbean area, which is prone to natural disasters. Thus he would be willing to accept reinsurance of business relating to risks in Europe.

▶ **To increase the capacity of the direct insurer.** Many direct insuring companies reinsure with Lloyd's, having accepted more of a risk than they are able to keep. They may also wish to increase their capacity to handle larger and more complex risks in various classes of business.

▶ **For financial reasons or to obtain technical advice from insurers** Many Lloyd's syndicates specialise in reinsurance and their expertise is used by direct insurers.

B

MAIN METHODS OF REINSURANCE

The main methods of reinsurance can be identified as follows:

Figure 2.2: Main methods of reinsurance

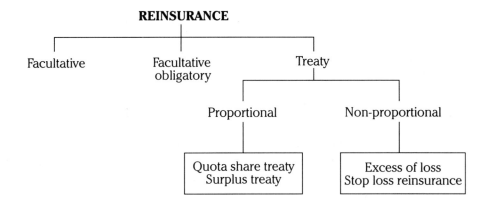

B1 FACULTATIVE

The earliest method of reinsurance used, and the most obvious, is simply to offer another insurer a portion of an individual risk where the amount accepted is too large for an insurer's own requirements. If the offer is accepted then a simple reinsurance policy is issued between the two parties.

◆**Facultative**◆ reinsurance is a method of reinsurance under which the ceding insurer (the reinsuring insurer) reinsures each risk individually. There is no obligation on the ◆**ceding insurer**◆ to reinsure any particular risk and it is at liberty to decide how much it will reinsure and how much it will retain for itself on any risk reinsured. The ceding insurer is at liberty to offer the reinsurance to any reinsurer it wishes. The prospective reinsurer is under no obligation to write any particular risk and can decline any risk and fix its share of any risk entirely as it sees fit.

Thus facultative reinsurance has some aspects similar to the underwriting of direct insurance; the ceding insurer taking the place of the insured, and the reinsurer taking the place of the direct insurer. It follows, therefore, that the reinsurer may require detailed underwriting information on each facultative reinsurance.

◆**Facultative obligatory**◆ reinsurance falls between facultative and treaty: whereas the ceding insurer can choose whether or not to ◆**cede**◆ to the reinsurer any risks falling within the terms of the agreement, the reinsurer is bound to accept automatically the business offered.

Q What are the disadvantages of the facultative method?

A The cost of reinsurance to the broker and reinsurer is high; placing may take a considerable time; and there is uncertainty until the reinsurance is arranged. Thus the ◆**treaty**◆ method of reinsurance evolved.

B2 TREATY

Treaty reinsurance is the method of reinsurance predominantly used. It is automatic and is an arrangement between one insurer (the ceding insurer) and a number of other insurers (the reinsurers) who agree to accept, automatically, any reinsurances (◆**cessions**◆) falling within the terms of the treaty.

The treaty sets out the various terms and conditions which are to govern the cessions (the amounts given off by way of reinsurance) and the acceptance of them by the reinsurer. A treaty is legally binding on both parties and both parties undertake obligations to each other which go beyond the mere ceding of individual risks or policies under the treaty.

The treaty cannot be cancelled except in accordance with the cancellation clause contained in it or both parties agree, or there is a breach of contract.

The main approaches to treaty reinsurance are proportional and non-proportional.

B2A Proportional reinsurance

Under this method of reinsurance, the direct insurer decides what proportion of the risk it wants to retain and then agrees to cede the balance to the reinsurers under the treaty. Premiums and losses are then shared in these same proportions. There are two types of proportional treaty, namely ◆**quota share treaty**◆ and ◆**surplus treaty**◆.

B2A1 Quota share treaty

The insurer agrees to pass on to the reinsurer a fixed proportion of all their acceptances (usually subject to a fixed upper limit) of business within the scope of the treaty.

The reinsurer receives a proportionate share of all premiums of the class and pays a proportionate share of all losses.

Example
Fire and allied lines business.
An insurer has a 75% quota share treaty up to a maximum of 75% of £1,000,000 any one risk. The reinsurer accepts 75% of all risks, and receives 75% of the premium, but only to a maximum amount of £750,000 (being 75% of £1,000,000). The ceding insurer must make separate arrangements if the risk is over £1,000,000.

	Risk 1	Risk 2	Risk 3
Sum insured	£10,000	£100,000	£1,300,000
Insurer's share	£2,500	£25,000	£250,000
Reinsurer's share	£7,500	£75,000	£750,000
Amount over treaty	Nil	Nil	£300,000

Q In the case of the last risk, the insurer would obtain further reinsurance either with a surplus treaty or on a facultative basis.

What do you feel is the main disadvantage of quota share reinsurance?

A The ceding insurer cannot vary retentions on individual risks. Surplus treaties allow him more freedom.

B2A2 Surplus treaty

The alternative to ceding a fixed proportion of every risk is for the direct insurer to decide how much of each risk it wants to retain for its own account. This amount is termed ◆**retention**◆ and is calculated on the expected financial loss.

The insurer agrees to pass on only the difference between the amount he has accepted and the amount he wishes to keep (retention), subject to a fixed upper limit.

The amount of the retention is also termed a ◆**line**◆ and a reinsurer may accept one or more lines or a fraction of a line.

An obligatory surplus treaty is an agreement between two parties under which, subject to the limitations of the agreement, the ceding insurer is obliged to cede on each and every risk it underwrites all liability surplus to its own retained line. The reinsurer is obliged to accept all such cessions. This is a logical development from facultative reinsurance. In practice, there will be several reinsurers all accepting part of the cession.

An obligatory surplus treaty is described as a first, second, third or even fourth obligatory surplus. A first surplus is used directly the ceding insurer's own net retention on a risk is exceeded. A second surplus is used when the first surplus is filled on a risk and third surplus when first and second are filled.

Example
An insurer effects a ten-line treaty with other insurers. This means that for every line he retains for his own account, he can reinsure up to ten such lines; in other words,

reinsurers automatically accept up to ten times his retention. For example:

Retention + Reinsurance = Acceptance
£5,000　　　£50,000　　　£55,000

These figures are based on a ten-line treaty. If it is necessary to accept more than £55,000 then only £50,000 can be placed with the treaty and facultative cover must be sought for the balance, unless there is a second treaty which will allow for further reinsurance.

B2B Non-proportional reinsurance

The proportional methods of reinsurance are concerned with proportions of the values at risk. The non-proportional methods are based on the losses, rather than the sums insured. The reinsurer agrees to pay an amount over and above, or in excess of, an amount which the direct insurer agrees to pay or retain.

B2B1 Excess of loss

The insurer decides the amount that he is prepared to bear on each and every loss, and arranges reinsurance to relieve him of any liability in excess of that amount, up to a limit.

The main attraction of ◆ **excess of loss** ◆ reinsurance is the protection that this can provide against catastrophic losses involving accumulations of net retentions (known as catastrophe excess of loss reinsurance). Catastrophe excess of loss reinsurance is essential where original coverage is granted for natural perils such as wind, storm, tempest, hurricane, earthquake, bush fires, etc., in order to prevent too great an exposure to any one event/disaster.

The aim of risk excess of loss reinsurance is to protect the reinsured for a loss involving only one risk. This can, in some cases, take the place of proportional reinsurance treaties, either because such cover would be unsuitable or even impossible.

Excess of loss programmes may well involve more than one layer of protection, particularly where the original business commands high limits or even unlimited cover such as employers' liability or motor. Each layer in such a programme would sit on top of the layer below, so that the complete programme would provide sufficient reinsurance protection, and take full advantage of the available market.

Example

Reinsured retention (retained loss), for example £100,000
1st Layer	£400,000	excess of	£100,000
2nd Layer	£500,000	excess of	£500,000
3rd Layer	£1,000,000	excess of	£1,000,000

B2B2 Stop loss (or excess of loss ratio)

By means of surplus or normal risk excess of loss reinsurance, the reinsured can reduce their net liability on individual risks to a figure well within their compass.

◆ **Stop loss** ◆ reinsurance is the form of protection which in those circumstances makes it possible to limit such ratio to an agreed percentage of the original insured's income on business protected, and it operates on the net retained lines of the original insurer.

The loss ratio of the original insurer is stopped at an agreed percentage and, if in any one calendar year the loss ratio exceeds that percentage, the reinsurer undertakes to pay the excess amount. The reinsurer will not give 'unlimited' cover, and will restrict liability to an agreed percentage of the net retained premium income and/or to a specified amount. Both limits are frequently inserted.

An example of a stop loss reinsurance could be for 90% of the amount in excess of a 70% loss ratio up to a further 50%. Thus reinsurers are liable for 90% of all losses after the loss ratio of the original insurer has reached 70% and until the loss ratio of the original insurer has reached 120%.

C

REINSURANCE PREMIUMS

The method of calculating reinsurance premiums is different for proportional and non-proportional reinsurances. The former are based on values at risk, whilst the latter, as we saw, are based on losses.

C1 PROPORTIONAL REINSURANCE PREMIUMS

For proportional reinsurance, losses and premiums are shared in the same proportion. However, the direct insurer may have paid survey costs and agents' commissions, whereas the reinsurer would not incur these costs. To compensate for this the reinsurer pays ceding commission to the direct insurer. On quota share treaties the ceding commission will equal the ceding insurer's original costs. On surplus treaties the commission will normally cover the ceding insurer's commission and other acquisition costs but will not cover the ceding insurer's overheads.

However, most treaties make some contribution to overheads by payment of an ◆**overriding comm-ission**◆ to the ceding insurer. A ◆**profit comm-ission**◆ based on the earned profits of the business passing under a reinsurance treaty may also be paid where the business is good.

C2 NON-PROPORTIONAL REINSURANCE PREMIUMS

In the case of non-proportional reinsurance, the eventual cost to the reinsurer is only known once the claims have been paid and this could be several years after the incident occurred.

The calculation of premium rates to be charged for non-proportional reinsurance is far more complex than those for proportional business. The reinsurer's intention behind the calculation of the rate is similar to that for rating direct business, namely to cover:

▶ the expected claims experience, including an allowance for incurred but not reported claims;

▶ the reinsurer's expenses;

▶ an allowance for a margin of profit and any other contingencies.

The actual calculation of rates is beyond the scope of this course. However, you should be aware that a minimum deposit premium may be charged, or a flat premium based on the expected original gross premium income of the ceding insurer. A risk excess of loss treaty may be rated on a loss cost or ◆**burning cost**◆ basis which adjusts the premium to be paid based on the paid and outstanding losses affecting the reinsurance contract.

SUMMARY

In this chapter we have examined the reasons for reinsurance and looked at the main types of reinsurance. In the next chapter we will consider the classes of risk covered at Lloyd's.

2

GLOSSARY OF TERMS

Burning cost
A method of calculating a reinsurance premium taking account of previous claims.

Cede
To transfer risk from a direct insurer to his reinsurers.

Ceding insurer (or cedant)
One who cedes a risk to his reinsurers or retrocessionaires.

Cessions
The particulars of a risk being transferred by one insurer to another.

Excess of loss
A reinsurance that covers that part of a loss paid by the reinsured which is in excess of an agreed amount and then pays up to the limit of the policy.

Fac/oblig
Facultative/obligatory. A reinsurance term for a contract where the reinsured can select which risks he cedes to the reinsurer, but the reinsruer is obliged to accept all cessions made.

Facultative
An individual reinsurance negotiated and placed individually.

Line (net)
The amount of the retention of the direct insurer; a reinsurer may accept one or more lines (or a fraction of a line).

Overriding commission
Commission payable in addition to the original commission.

Profit commission
A commission payable on the profit generated under an insurance or reinsurance contract as an encouragement to maintain the flow of profitable business.

Quota share treaty
A reinsurance agreement whereby the reinsured cedes a predetermined proportion of all business (or specified part thereof) to his reinsurers.

Reinsurance (R/I)
The reinsurance of an insured risk. The 'laying-off' of a risk by an insurer to protect his particular liability and to maintain liquidity.

Retention

The amount retained by a reinsured when effecting reinsurance.

Retrocession

The 'laying-off' of liability accepted by way of reinsurance for the same reasons as reinsurance.

Stop loss (excess of loss ratio)

A form of protection which makes it possible to limit the loss ratio on a year of account to an agreed percentage of the original insured's premium income on business protected. Personal stop loss reinsurances are also used by individual members to obtain a measure of protection against an overall underwriting loss on any one year of account.

Surplus treaty or surplus line

A reinsurance where the surplus of the reinsured's retention is ceded up to an agreed amount. The reinsurers will normally base this participation on the retention of the ceding insurer but, once accepted, the reinsured and the reinsurers pay their proportion of losses arising.

Treaty

A reinsurance contract usually effected to cover the whole or a certain section of the reinsured's business.

2

MULTIPLE CHOICE QUESTIONS

1. When an underwriter takes out a reinsurance on a risk, who will pay the original claims should one or more of the reinsurers go into liquidation?

    (a) The other underwriters who accepted the original risk.
    (b) The Corporation of Lloyd's via the central fund.
    (c) The Insurance Division of the Department of Trade and Industry.
    (d) The names on the syndicate of the underwriter who first insured the risk.

2. Individual risks for reinsurance, submitted individually to reinsurers, are termed:

    (a) facultative business;
    (b) first loss business;
    (c) ceded business;
    (d) surplus business.

3. A facultative obligatory reinsurance contract means that:

    (a) the ceding underwriter can choose whether or not to cede risks: the reinsurer is obliged to accept cessions made within the terms of the agreement;

    (b) the ceding underwriter is bound to cede any risk within the terms of the agreement and the reinsurer is bound to accept;

    (c) the reinsurer is free to accept or decline risks offered to him;

    (d) both parties may choose whether or not to bind each other, within the terms of the agreement.

4. On a particular type of risk a syndicate has a retention of £40,000. It has a four-line surplus treaty. The broker wishes to cover a factory for £400,000. How much of the risk can the syndicate accept without further reinsurance arrangements being made?

    (a) £40,000.
    (b) £160,000.
    (c) £200,000.
    (d) £400,000.

2

MULTIPLE CHOICE QUESTIONS

5.   An underwriter has a four-line surplus treaty. He is approached to insure a direct risk and is asked for a line of £600,000. His retention for this class of risk is £100,000. What maximum line will he be able to write without making separate reinsurance arrangements?

   (a)   £100,000.
   (b)   £500,000.
   (c)   £600,000.
   (d)   £3,000,000.

6.   An underwriter effects a six-line treaty with a reinsurer. This means that he can write a line equal to a multiple of the amount he keeps for his own account without making separate reinsurance arrangements.

   This multiple is:

   (a)   six;
   (b)   seven;
   (c)   eight;
   (d)   twelve.

ANSWERS TO MULTIPLE CHOICE QUESTIONS APPEAR OVERLEAF

ANSWERS TO MULTIPLE CHOICE QUESTIONS

1. Answer (d), the names on the syndicate of the underwriter who first insured the risk.

2. Answer (a), facultative business.

3. Answer (a), the ceding underwriter can choose whether or not to cede risks: the reinsurer is obliged to accept cessions made within the terms of the agreement.

4. Answer (c), £200,000.

5. Answer (b), £500,000.

6. Answer (b), the multiple is seven.

3

CLASSES OF BUSINESS AT LLOYD'S

A Marine insurance

B Non-marine insurance

C Motor insurance

D Aviation insurance

INTRODUCTION

In chapter 1 we saw that the first class of insurance to be introduced to Britain was marine insurance. Other forms of insurance developed over the centuries as demand grew, and the classes of insurance written by Lloyd's underwriters reflects this historical development. The merchants in Lloyd's coffee house were carrying on purely marine insurance and this developed, when Lloyd's was formed as a Society, to include non-marine insurance. From this developed motor and, latterly, aviation insurance.

In this chapter we will review the main classes of business transacted at Lloyd's.

Business at Lloyd's is often termed ◆**long tail**◆ or ◆**short tail**◆:

▶ Long tail business is the term used to describe a risk that may have claims notified or settled long after the risk has expired. Thus, it is often necessary for a syndicate to arrange reinsurance protection to cover claims which arise after the account has been closed. The term may also be used to describe liability risks rather than those for physical damage.

▶ Short tail business is the term used to describe a risk where all claims are likely to arise and be settled within the policy period or shortly afterwards.

LEARNING OBJECTIVES

After studying this chapter, you should be able to:

▷ list and discuss the main classes of risks written at Lloyd's;

▷ identify the main forms of cover given under each class;

▷ outline the losses and liabilities which may give rise to claims under each class;

▷ examine the main methods of reinsurance suitable for each class.

A

MARINE INSURANCE

Marine insurance is an essential feature of trade, particularly overseas trade. Lloyd's occupies a leading place in the world marine insurance market. Marine insurance has its own terminology and is the only class to have terms defined within an Act of Parliament, the **Marine Insurance Act 1906** (MIA 1906).

A1 SCOPE OF MARINE INSURANCE

Marine insurance provides an indemnity against the majority of losses which can occur during a maritime transit, and may extend to losses on inland waters and on land. The MIA 1906 was an Act to codify the law to that date. (The Act refers to a 'marine adventure'.)

A2 WHO MAY INSURE

Anyone who has an ◆**insurable interest**◆ in a 'marine adventure' may insure; for example shipowners, charterers, parties interested in monies (freight, passage money, profit, etc.) where the insured property may be endangered by maritime ◆**perils**◆ and those exposed to liabilities to third parties, which may arise by reason of maritime perils.

Insurers may reinsure their interest. Master and crew have an insurable interest in their wages. The cost of insurance (premiums) may be insured. Cargo owners have an interest, as do owners of property involved in the offshore oil and gas industry.

A3 PERIOD OF COVER

Ships and freight are insured for a period of time or for a voyage or 'mixed time,' i.e. time and voyage. Cargo is insured for the voyage and frequently warehouse to warehouse. The cover for cargo risks is usually limited to 60 days after discharge from the vessel.

'Floating policies' are taken out for an agreed sum sufficiently large to cover a number of shipments, each shipment being declared by the insured. Cargo risks may also be insured for a fixed period of time and open covers, which are agreements stating in general terms the conditions under which future policies for specified goods will be issued, are also written.

Builders' risks are insured during construction ashore, trials and until the vessel is delivered by the builder to the shipowner.

Drilling rigs and platforms are insured for construction, the voyage to the site, placing on the site, further construction until the complex is completed and thereafter.

A4 COVERAGE AND INSURED PERILS

In marine insurance a standard policy form is used but the cover given is contained in clauses attached to the policy.

A4A Standard MAR form

The standard MAR form is used for hull, cargo and freight risks, with appropriate detailed clauses attached. The clauses are termed ◆**Institute clauses**◆, which refers to the Institute of London Underwriters, the company marine association. However, the clauses are drafted by joint committees of Lloyd's and company underwriters. Underwriters may occasionally agree to use of the previous SG (Ship Goods) form of policy.

A4B Hull clauses

The standard clauses show 'named perils' covered by the policy and cover loss of or damage to the subject matter insured caused by:

Peril of the seas rivers lakes or other navigable waters, fire, explosion, violent theft by persons from outside the vessel, jettison, piracy, breakdown or accident to nuclear installations or reactors, contact with aircraft or similar objects, or objects falling therefrom, land conveyance, dock or harbour equipment or installation, earthquake, volcanic eruption or lightning.

Additionally, the insurance covers:

loss of damage to the subject matter insured caused by accidents in loading discharging or shifting cargo or fuel, bursting of boilers, breaking of shafts or any latent defect in the machinery or hull, negligence of Master Officers Crew or Pilots, negligence of repairers or chart-

erers provided such repairers or charterers are not an Assured hereunder, barratry of Master Officers or Crew, provided such loss or damage has not resulted from want of due diligence by the *Assured, Owners or Managers.

*The terms assured and insured have the same meaning.

The policy extends to cover three-quarters of the liability for damage caused to another vessel by collision and three-quarters of the cost of defending any action or limiting liabilities. There are various other options available to cover the remaining quarter.

The policy is subject to a ◆**deductible**◆.

These clauses are intended for use with the MAR form of policy. Other wordings are used for the previous SG policy.

A4C Cargo clauses

The Institute Cargo Clauses (A) cover 'all risks' of loss or damage due to a fortuity, excluding loss or damage caused by stated exclusions; therefore, they offer the widest cover.

The two remaining sets cover named perils only, i.e. they name precisely what is and what is not covered and (Institute clauses B and C). The Institute Cargo Clauses (C) provide the basic standard cover against major casualties and clauses (B) offer wider cover than (C).

These clauses are intended for use with the MAR form of policy.

A4D Freight insurance

The cover is for the sum paid for transporting goods or for hire of a vessel.

A5 CLAIMS

Losses in marine insurance are separated into two main categories, total losses and partial losses. We will consider each category independently.

A5A Total loss

Any loss other than a total loss is defined as a partial loss and is treated as such.

A total loss may either be an actual total loss or a constructive total loss.

An ◆**actual total loss**◆ may occur where the subject matter insured is destroyed or so damaged as to cease to be a thing of the kind insured (for example, cement so wetted that it is turned to concrete) or where the insured is irretrievably deprived of his property (for example, a vessel is seized by the government of a country as a political act).

The second kind of total loss, ◆**constructive total loss**◆, presents greater difficulties than actual total loss, but is better understood if it is recognised that an actual total loss is a physical total loss. There can be no doubt about this loss; it is absolute.

A constructive total loss (CTL) can be considered as a 'commercial' total loss. It implies that the subject matter is not destroyed, and is not totally lost, but commercially a total loss has occurred.

Constructive total loss is defined in the MIA 1906 as a loss which occurs where the subject matter of the insurance is reasonably abandoned by the insured on account of its actual total loss appearing unavoidable or because it could not be preserved from actual total loss without expenditure that would exceed its value after the expense has been incurred. The Act specifically states the right of the insured to claim as a partial loss, or abandon the subject matter insured to the insurer and claim for CTL. It also outlines the method of giving notice of abandonment; if the notice of abandonment is accepted, the abandonment is irrevocable.

In practice, insurers generally decline the notice of abandonment, although, after payment of the claim, they are entitled to take over the interest of the insured in what is left of the subject matter insured.

A5B Partial loss

The word 'average' in marine insurance has a different meaning from that used in other branches of property insurance. The term is similar to 'partial loss'. However, the meaning of average is slightly different when used in connection with general average. A general average loss may involve total loss of one particular subject matter, but it is still a partial loss in relation to the whole 'adventure' (which means voyage). Again, the term general average includes expenditure in connection with a general average act, whereas ◆**particular average**◆ includes only loss.

A5B1 General average

There is a ◆**general average**◆ act where any extraordinary sacrifice or expenditure is **voluntarily and reasonably** made or incurred in time of peril for the purpose of preserving the property imperilled in the common adventure, and the whole of the property thereby preserved shall contribute to the loss sustained or expenditure incurred.

General average arises irrespective of insurance and, provided the general average contribution arises from a peril insured against, a claim would be recoverable

under the policy (under-insurance would reduce the claim).

Example
In a heavy storm, a vessel is in danger of capsizing. In order to save his vessel, the master can declare a general average and order the jettisoning of all his deck cargo.

Where general average is declared, all interested parties (and this would include the owner of the sacrificed goods) bear a share of the loss, so that the owner of the goods sacrificed is not unduly prejudiced.

The phrase 'common adventure' is used as general average even pre-dates marine insurance itself, thus the principle has existed for hundreds of years.

General average is thus a partial loss, but it refers to a loss that is shared by all parties involved in the voyage, and does not merely fall upon the owners of the goods lost in our example. Any sacrifice or expenditure must save the 'adventure' for general average to operate.

A5B2 Particular average

Particular average is a partial loss of, or damage to, the subject matter insured, caused by a peril insured against, which is not a general average loss.

It is obvious that particular average covers a very wide range of losses, and it may be damage to, or loss of part of, the subject matter insured. The essential feature is that loss or damage must have been accidentally and fortuitously caused by an insured peril.

Figure 3.1

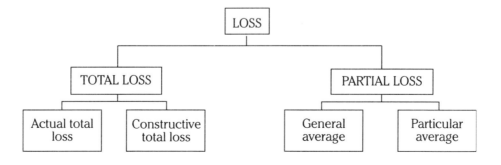

A6 SALVAGE CHARGES

These are the charges recoverable under maritime law by a salvor independently of contract, i.e. by a voluntary third party salvor successfully saving maritime property in peril at sea.

Provided the salvage arose from the operation of an insured peril, there would be right of recovery under the insurance. (Again, any under-insurance would reduce the claim.)

A7 PARTICULAR CHARGES

Underwriters pay charges incurred by the insured in an effort to avert or minimise losses which would be recoverable under the insurance. These are often termed ◆**sue and labour charges**◆, being the phrase used in the old SG form of marine policy.

A8 MARINE REINSURANCE

Many Lloyd's underwriters now underwrite the reinsurance protection of other syndicates and insurance companies based in the UK and abroad (this is often referred to as 'inward' or 'assumed' reinsurance).

This business is written in any of the various ways mentioned in chapter 2 and, in total, 'assumed' reinsurance now constitutes a major part of any marine underwriter's portfolio of business.

The basic division that any marine underwriter will make regarding excess of loss business is between reinsurance from abroad and reinsurance of London market underwriters; the latter commonly known as **LMX**.

The facultative reinsurance will be placed either on original conditions or limited conditions such as **TLO (total loss only)**.

Any contract reinsurance will be subject to a contract wording (whether proportional or non-proportional) which, when signed, will be the legal document reinforcing the terms of the slip. Until such time as the contract wording is signed, the slip remains as the legal embodiment of the contract.

NON-MARINE INSURANCE

Lloyd's widened its scope when the first non-marine risks were accepted from broking firms whose marine risks had been placed at Lloyd's. The main non-marine classes of business are considered in the following sections and include insurance of property, liability and the person.

B1 FIRE INSURANCE

The Lloyd's fire policy covers fire and/or lightning, fire consequent upon explosion wherever explosion occurs, explosion consequent upon fire on the premises insured and explosion of domestic boilers and/or gas used for domestic purposes or for heating and/or lightning.

The policy contains a ◆**pro rata average**◆ condition which is applied where there is under-insurance. Under-insurance is unfair to the insurer in as much as he does not receive the correct premium for the risk he is running. This will produce an unduly adverse loss experience and may then lead to a general increase in rates which will have to be borne by all insured in the category concerned. Under-insurance thus becomes unfair to other policyholders where some insured fail to make their fair contribution to the insurer's fund.

Because of the adverse effect of under-insurance on claims experience, the pro rata average clause is incorporated. This provision is designed to ensure equitable treatment between those who insure for the full value of their property and those who are under-insured.

Example
The owner of a factory insures his property for £300,000 and pays the premium reflecting that sum insured. The building catches fire and sustains damage to the amount of £100,000.

The insurers calculate that the true value of the property is in fact £400,000; therefore, the property is under-insured. The insurers have only received a premium which reflects three-quarters of the property's true value. Therefore, they will only pay three - quarters of the claim:

$$\frac{\text{Sum insured}}{\text{Value at risk at time of loss}} \times \text{loss} = \text{Claim payment}$$

$$\frac{£300,000}{£400,000} \times £100,000 = £75,000$$

B1A Additional perils

Additional perils may be added to the fire policy at an additional premium. These may be classified as follows:

▶ chemical perils; for example, explosion;

▶ social perils; for example, riot, civil commotion and malicious damage;

▶ natural perils; for example, storm, tempest, flood, earthquake;

▶ miscellaneous perils; for example, burst pipes and water damage, aircraft or other aerial devices or articles dropped therefrom, impact by vehicles, horses or cattle of third party, sprinkler leakage.

B1B Business interruption insurance

The fire insurance policy covering material damage makes no provision for loss of earnings or additional expenses incurred in maintaining or re-establishing the business after damage.

A fire in business premises can cause serious interruption or dislocation to the business, resulting in diminution of trade during a period following the damage, and certain standing charges might still be required to be paid even though the business may be entirely stopped for a period.

The business interruption policy covers reduction in profit due to the reduction in the volume of trade as a result of the damage and increase in the cost of working.

B2 THEFT INSURANCE

Theft policies have the same aim as the fire policy in that they provide compensation to the insured in the event of loss of the property insured.

The law relating to theft was brought up-to-date by the **Theft Act 1968** which defined the term theft. This legal definition was wider than the cover desired to be provided by underwriters. Underwriters qualify the Act's wording and cover loss of or damage to property within the premises by theft or attempted theft following entry or exit from the premises by forcible and violent means.

B3 MONEY INSURANCE

The policy covers loss of money (which also includes a wide range of notes, cheques, bankers drafts, stamps, tokens, vouchers, etc.) in transit, on specified premises and in a bank night safe. The policy may be extended, at an additional premium, to cover bodily injury arising from theft of money.

B4 JEWELLERS' BLOCK INSURANCE

The policy covers stock and merchandise used in the conduct of the insured's business and bank notes against any loss or damage from any cause whatsoever whilst in territorial limits. The policy also covers premises, trade and office fixtures, fittings, etc., against a wide range of perils. The policy contains strict limits for certain losses specified in the policy.

B5 HOME INSURANCE

The policy covers buildings and contents against a comprehensive list of perils including fire, additional perils, theft and public liability.

B6 GOODS IN TRANSIT INSURANCE

The policy provides 'all risks' cover for property being loaded onto, carried on or unloaded from motor vehicles and trailers, including temporary garaging during the transit in the United Kingdom. The policy may be extended to rail, post or other forms of transit.

B7 BANKERS' BLANKET POLICY

Providing policy cover for all insurance needs of banks is commonly known as a 'bond'. The policy covers:

► fidelity;
► premises cover;
► transit of cash and valuables by employees;
► forgery;
► counterfeit currency loss;
► damage to office and contents.

The policy may be extended to cover:

► computer fraud;
► safe deposit box liability;
► kidnap and ransom.

B8 BUILDERS' AND CONTRACTORS' INSURANCE

This form of insurance arose from the growth in civil engineering projects both at home and abroad. The policy covers physical damage from a wide range of perils and public liability risks for the construction and erection and the maintenance period.

B9 PACKAGE POLICIES

These policies provide broader and more satisfactory cover than single policies. A typical policy would provide cover for the following:

► fire and additional perils;
► theft;
► loss of profit;
► money;
► goods in transit;
► personal accident;
► fidelity (a guarantee of someone's honesty);
► glass;

► book debts;
► engineering;
► legal liabilities.

B10 PERSONAL ACCIDENT INSURANCE

The policy pays compensation for death or injury by accident.

Normally, the maximum capital is paid for death with a sliding scale of benefits for permanent or temporary disablement.

B11 ACCIDENT AND ILLNESS INSURANCE

The policy cover is as for the accident policy. However, in addition, capital sums are payable for permanent total loss of sight of both eyes and permanent total disablement by illness of any kind.

B12 PUBLIC LIABILITY (THIRD PARTY) INSURANCE

The policy provides an indemnity to the insured against legal ♦**liability**♦ at law for damages paid to claimants for bodily injury or disease (fatal or non-fatal) or damage to property. The policy covers both the claimants' and the insured's costs and expenses.

B13 ERRORS AND OMISSIONS

The policy covers liability for professional ♦**negligence**♦ causing financial or personal injury to clients. The insured include, for example, the following:

► accountants;
► chemists;
► druggists;
► doctors;
► dentists;
► surgeons;
► insurance brokers;

▶ solicitors;
▶ stockbrokers.

B14 PRODUCTS LIABILITY INSURANCE

The policy covers legal liability for bodily injury or property damage which arises out of goods or products (including food and drink) manufactured, constructed, altered, repaired, serviced, treated, sold, supplied or distributed by the insured.

B15 EMPLOYERS' LIABILITY INSURANCE

The policy covers legal liability for damages if any person under contract of service or apprenticeship sustains bodily injury or disease or death resulting therefrom arising out of and in course of employment by the insured. Insurance is compulsory for all but a few employers. An annual certificate is issued, copies of which must be displayed at every place of business as evidence of the fact that the employer has complied with the law and effected a policy.

B16 LIVESTOCK INSURANCE

This covers the insured against death of animals as a result of accident, illness or disease.

B17 LIFE ASSURANCE

Short-term contracts not exceeding ten years in duration are written by specialist life syndicates. The sum assured is payable on death if it occurs within the policy term.

B18 NON-MARINE REINSURANCE

A large part of the portfolio of business underwritten in the non-marine market is inwards reinsurance (reinsurance coming into Lloyd's from outside insurers).

Non-marine business by definition normally gives protection within the territorial limits of an individual country.

Local legislation frequently requires that insurances should be placed with locally registered or national companies. This domestic market inevitably needs reinsurance to cover large and unusual risks and to give protection against catastrophic losses.

Lloyd's has, since the nineteenth century, enjoyed a major share of the reinsurance business placed by the United States domestic market. Proportional treaty and facultative reinsurances covering most of the major classes of business come into the market. Most of these placings involve both an American and a Lloyd's broker.

Excess of loss reinsurance has found a natural home at Lloyd's since the first reinsurance of this nature was written by Cuthbert Heath soon after the San Francisco earthquake of 1906. The benefits of excess of loss protection have now spread worldwide and Lloyd's remains a prime market for this business from every country. The construction of new contracts employing simple or sometimes complex rating formulas that depend upon the contract experience has been a feature of this class of business.

C

MOTOR INSURANCE

The minimum requirement by law is to provide insurance in respect of legal liability to pay damages arising out of injury caused to any person or damage to third party property under the **Road Traffic Acts 1988** and **1991**. Let us begin by considering the four classes of risk in respect of motor insurance.

C1 CLASSES OF RISK

Underwriters insure the following classes of risk:

▶ private cars;
▶ motor cycles;
▶ commercial vehicles;
▶ motor trade risks.

C1A Private cars

This class covers private cars used for private and business purposes (other than the carriage of passengers for hire or reward). Goods-carrying vehicles used solely for private purposes are usually rated as private cars.

C1B Motor cycles

In insurance the term 'motor cycle' includes any kind of cycle propelled mechanically and includes mopeds. Consequently, there is a wide range of risk.

C1C Commercial vehicles

This covers the following commercial vehicles (including private cars carrying passengers for hire or reward):

- ▶ goods-carrying vehicles;
- ▶ hire cars, taxis, coaches and buses;
- ▶ agricultural and forestry vehicles;
- ▶ miscellaneous vehicles usually known as 'special types'; for example, ambulances, mobile plant and excavators, mobile shops, fork-lift trucks, etc.

C1D Motor trade risks

This class covers motor trade risks, including vehicles used by or in the care, custody and control of motor traders. Motor trade risks may also cover the internal or premises risks of the motor trader.

Cover for the motor trader is not limited to specified vehicles or specified drivers. A motor trader requires to be covered in respect of vehicles which pass through his hands by way of trade, either for sale or repair, in addition to vehicles that he owns. The policy may cover driving by customers.

C2 MOTOR POLICIES

A comprehensive policy offers the widest form of cover. However, despite its name, it does not cover every type of risk.

The policy provides a range of other benefits which are not provided by other motor policies giving more restricted cover.

C2A The comprehensive policy

A typical policy will cover:

- ▶ loss of or damage to insured's vehicles and accessories and spare parts thereon by:

  - fire and theft,
  - accidental damage,
  - malicious damage,
  - frost (except motor cycles);

- ▶ ◆**third party liabilities**◆, including passenger liability;
- ▶ liability of passengers;
- ▶ personal accident benefits;
- ▶ loss of rugs, clothing and personal effects;
- ▶ medical expenses;
- ▶ emergency treatment.

} in respect of private cars

The policy may also be extended to cover, for example:

- ▶ legal costs for manslaughter or reckless or dangerous driving causing death;
- ▶ breakage of windscreen and windows;
- ▶ legal liability to paid driver for accident;
- ▶ loss of use;
- ▶ cost of delivery to insured in the UK following accident;
- ▶ foreign use;
- ▶ fire damage to garage;
- ▶ loss of road fund licence;
- ▶ towing of trailer or caravan.

} in respect of private cars

There is a wide range of policy covers within the Lloyd's market and various syndicates will offer other extensions of cover.

C2B Restricted cover

Underwriters also offer third party and third party, fire and theft cover.

A **third party only** policy covers liability for death or bodily injury to a third party and liability for damage to third party property. This will include pedestrians, passengers in other cars, passengers in the policyholder's care and other third party cars or property.

A **third party, fire and theft** policy covers third party risks as with the 'third party only' policy, plus the risks of fire and theft.

Figure 3.2: Types of motor insurance cover

Third party only	**Third party, fire and theft**	**Comprehensive**
Death of, or bodily injury to, any person and damage to third party property.	Third party cover	Third party, fire and theft cover
	plus	plus
	fire and/or theft, loss or damage to the vehicle by fire or theft.	Other accidental loss or damage to the vehicle plus additional benefits.

C3 MOTOR REINSURANCE

Reinsurance cover normally will be on an excess of loss treaty basis.

Large personal injury claims from third parties may arise from any accident. Policies issued under the Road Traffic Act 1988 give unlimited indemnity for personal injury claims.

D
AVIATION INSURANCE

The use of aircraft as a means of transport is increasing each year and, because of the specialist and technical nature of the risks associated with it, plus the high potential cost of accidents, all aviation risks (from component parts to complete jumbo jets) are insured.

The buyers of these policies include the large commercial airlines, corporate aircraft owners, private owners and flying clubs.

Certain liability risks are governed by international conventions.

D1 THE LLOYD'S AVIATION POLICY

The standard aircraft policy cover is as follows:

▶ Section 1. Loss or damage to the aircraft.
▶ Section 2. Legal liability to third parties other than passengers.
▶ Section 3. Legal liability to passengers.

D1A Loss or damage to the aircraft

The policy will pay for, replace or repair accidental loss or damage to the aircraft arising from risks covered, including disappearance if unreported 60 days after commencement of flight. The policy will also pay reasonable emergency expenses up to 10% of the sum insured.

The policy excludes ♦**wear and tear**♦, breakdown and damage which has a progressive or cumulative effect.

D1B Legal liability to third parties other than passengers

The policy covers legal liability and agreed law costs for bodily injury or damage to property, subject to limits for each person and each accident.

D1C Legal liability to passengers

The policy covers legal liability and agreed costs in respect of claims from passengers for injury or damage to, or loss of, personal effects and baggage, subject to limits for each passenger and each aircraft.

D2 OTHER FORMS OF COVER

A wide range of other risks are insured. These include:

▶ **Products legal liability**. The policy covers the legal liability of manufacturers or repairers.

▶ **Airport liability**. The policy covers the legal liability of airport operators for claims for bodily injury or damage.

▶ **Cargo**. The policy gives 'all risks' cover for the whole of the transit.

▶ **Loss of licence**. This covers aircrew who lose their licences in the event of being unfit through accident or illness.

▶ **Loss of use**. This policy covers loss of earnings following an aircraft being laid-up for repairs.

▶ **Personal accident**. Policies may be effected by passengers or aircrew for their own benefit. Group policies are issued on a declaration basis. Automatic personal accident cover may be provided by firms for their passengers.

▶ **Satellite risks**. The policy covers material damage during testing, launch or while in orbit and may cover loss of revenue.

D3 AVIATION REINSURANCE

The main forms of reinsurance used in the aviation insurance business fall under the following headings:

▶ facultative reinsurance;
▶ excess of loss treaties;
▶ quota share treaties;
▶ surplus treaties;
▶ facultative obligatory covers.

The risks covered are hull and the various legal liabilities.

SUMMARY

In this chapter we have examined the main classes of business transacted at Lloyd's. We have covered a vast amount of material but we must note that the various covers we have looked at probably contain ♦**exclusions**♦ which we have not detailed.

In the next chapter we will examine the legal principles which govern the transaction of insurance at Lloyd's, including basic contract law.

3

GLOSSARY OF TERMS

Actual total loss

There is an actual total loss where the subject matter of insurance is completely destroyed or so damaged as to cease to be a thing of the kind insured, or where the insured is irretrievably deprived of it.

Clauses

- ▶ Sections of a policy or other legal document.
- ▶ In marine insurance, sets of detailed provisions inserted for particular types of risk.

Constructive total loss

In marine insurance a constructive total loss occurs where the subject matter of insurance is reasonably abandoned by the insured on account of its actual total loss appearing unavoidable or because it could not be preserved from actual total loss without expenditure that would exceed its value after the expense had been incurred.

Deductible

An amount or percentage, specified in a policy, which is deducted from the total amount of the claim made. Otherwise known as 'excess'; this being the first portion of a loss, being an agreed percentage or fixed sum, which the insured agrees to bear or a portion another insurer is bearing.

Exclusion

A provision in a policy that excludes the insurer's liability in certain circumstances or for specified types of loss.

General average (loss)

In maritime law when, in a maritime venture, a sacrifice has to be made or an expense incurred in time of peril in order to preserve the venture, the loss or expense is shared among the interests involved in the venture in proportion to the value of each interest. Such a loss is known as a general average loss.

Insurable interest

The insured's financial interest in the subject matter of the insurance. A policy where the insured is without such interest is unenforceable.

Liability insurance

Insurance to cover the legal liability of the insured to the extent of such liability but subject to any limitations expressed in the policy.

Long tail

A term used to describe a risk that may have claims notified or settled long after the risk has expired. So that he can close the underwriting account for the year, it is often necessary for an underwriter to arrange reinsurance protection to cover claims which may arise after the account has been closed. A term used to describe risk covered as those of liability rather than physical damage.

Negligence

The omission to do something which a reasonable man, guided by those considerations which ordinarily regulate the conduct of human affairs, would do, or doing something which a prudent and reasonable man would not do.

Particular average (loss)

Partial loss or damage to the subject matter insured, caused by a peril insured against, not being a general average loss.

Peril

A contingency, or fortuitous happening, which may be covered or excluded by a policy of insurance.

Pro rata condition of average

A policy condition providing that in the event of under-insurance any claim shall be scaled down in proportion to the degree of under-insurance.

Short tail

A term used to describe a risk in respect of which all claims are likely to be advised and settled within the period of cover or shortly after the cover has expired. Normally confined to physical damage risks.

Sue and labour (charges)

Sums reimbursable to an insured under a marine insurance policy where the insured has incurred reasonable expense in seeking to avert or minimise a loss to property which would have been covered by the policy had the loss occurred.

Third party liability

Liability incurred by the insured to another party under common or statute law.

Wear and tear

This is the amount deducted from claims payments to allow for any depreciation in the property insured which is caused by its usage.

3

MULTIPLE CHOICE QUESTIONS

1. In marine insurance, the letters CTL mean:

   (a) cargo total liability;
   (b) cargo total loss;
   (c) constructive total loss;
   (d) constructive total liability.

2. The phrase 'sue and labour' means:

   (a) legal action taken against a crew guilty of acts of barratry;
   (b) legal redress open to insurers to minimise losses caused by negligence on part of insured;
   (c) payment of charges incurred by insured in effort to avert or minimise recoverable losses;
   (d) payment of legal charges incurred by insured in actions brought against negligent employees.

3. The voluntary jettison of cargo in an attempt to save a ship in peril is:

   (a) particular average;
   (b) uninsurable;
   (c) general average;
   (d) pro rata condition of average.

4. Following a claim for fire damage to the insured's property, the insurer establishes that the property has been under-insured. The property was insured for £80,000 when its true value was £100,000.

   Assuming the damage resulted in a loss of £50,000, how much will the insurer pay?

   (a) £35,000.
   (b) £40,000.
   (c) £45,000.
   (d) £50,000.

5.   Which policy specifically covers loss of profits?

    (a)   Fire policy.
    (b)   Money policy.
    (c)   Business interruption policy.
    (d)   Bankers blanket policy.

6.   Third party liability is the legal liability:

    (a)   of an insurer to its reinsurers;
    (b)   incurred by the insured to another party;
    (c)   of a broker to the underwriter;
    (d)   of an employer to his employees.

7.   Additional perils cover may be added to which of the following policies?

    (a)   Fire.
    (b)   Theft.
    (c)   Public liability.
    (d)   Employer's liability.

8.   How are the main classes of risk in motor insurance split?

    (a)   Public transport, private transport and military vehicles.
    (b)   Private cars, motor cycles, commercial, motor trade risks and comprehensive policies.
    (c)   Private cars, motor cycles, commercial and comprehensive policies.
    (d)   Private cars, motor cycles, commercial and motor trade risks.

9.   Motor trade risks cover vehicles used by motor traders. Which of the following risks may also be covered by the policy?

(a)   Business interruption.
(b)   Fidelity guarantee.
(c)   Internal or premises risks.
(d)   Loss of licence.

10.   An engine cowling falls from an airliner coming into Heathrow. It causes considerable damage to the roof of a private house in Hounslow. In which section of the standard aircraft policy would you look to find out what insurance cover the airline has against claims arising from the incident?

(a)   The declaration of exclusions.
(b)   Section 2.
(c)   Section 3.
(d)   Standard aircraft policy appendix 1.

3

ANSWERS TO MULTIPLE CHOICE QUESTIONS

1. Answer (c), constructive total loss.

2. Answer (c), payment of charges incurred by the insured in an effort to avert or minimise losses recoverable under the insurance.

3. Answer (c), general average.

4. Answer (b), £40,000.

    $$\frac{£80,000}{£100,000} \times £50,000 = £40,000$$

5. Answer (c), business interruption policy.

6. Answer (b), incurred by the insured to another party.

7. Answer (a), the fire policy.

8. Answer (d), private cars, motor cycles, commercial and motor trade risks.

9. Answer (c), internal or premises risks.

10. Answer (b), the correct section to look under would be Section 2 which deals with legal liability to third parties other than passengers.

4

LEGAL PRINCIPLES

A Contract law

B Utmost good faith

C Insurable interest

D Indemnity

E Subrogation

F Contribution

G Proximate cause

H Warranties

LEARNING OBJECTIVES

After studying this chapter, you should be able to:

▷ discuss the legal principles governing insurance transactions;

▷ explain the significance of utmost good faith in the relationship between underwriter and broker;

▷ identify the purpose and effect of warranties;

▷ write brief notes on the essential elements of the law of contract.

INTRODUCTION

◆**Insurance contracts**◆ transacted at Lloyd's are subject not only to the rules of basic contract law but also to legal principles which govern the transaction of insurance business as a whole. The main principles relate to the duty of the insured to tell the truth about the risk to be insured, to have the legal right to insure, not to make a profit from a loss covered under the policy and to be able to claim only when the loss was caused by a peril insured by the policy.

In this chapter we will examine these legal principles. Understanding the legal principles governing insurance transactions is essential to an understanding of how the Lloyd's market works.

A

CONTRACT LAW

A contract is a legally binding agreement between two or more parties. The policy of insurance is the evidence of the contract. Contracts may be **simple** or **specialty** contracts (or deeds). The great majority of insurance contracts are simple contracts. There is no necessity for simple contracts to be in writing; however, in practice, insurance contracts are evidenced in writing and S.22 of the Marine Insurance Act 1906 requires marine insurance contracts to be in writing. To constitute a valid contract the parties to it must have intended their agreement to give rise to legal obligations.

A1 ESSENTIAL ELEMENTS OF CONTRACTS

There are seven essential elements of simple contracts. These are as follows:

- ▶ capacity;
- ▶ legality;
- ▶ possibility;
- ▶ offer;
- ▶ acceptance;
- ▶ *consensus ad idem*;
- ▶ consideration.

A1A Capacity

Both parties must be capable of entering into a legally enforceable agreement. However, some classes of person have limited capacity to contract in law. These include statutory corporations where the contract must be in accordance with the object for which the corporation was created, or else it is *ultra vires* and void.

A1B Legality

The parties must intend to enter into a legal relationship. The subject matter of the contract must not be contrary to law (for instance, a marine cargo policy with an enemy national in time of war).

A1C Possibility

The performance of the contract must be possible in fact and in law.

A1D Offer

There must be an unrevoked offer by one party to another or others. The offer may be written, verbal or by conduct and it must be communicated. The offer is usually made by the proposer and contained in a duly completed proposal form completed by the prospective insured or is contained in the written details on the slip shown to underwriters.

The issue of a proposal form by insurers does not itself constitute an offer. It is simply an invitation to a prospective insured to offer an insurance which the insurer may accept or reject or agree on certain terms only.

A1E Acceptance

The acceptance must be unqualified and must coincide exactly with the offer. It may be written, verbal or by conduct and must generally be communicated, and is open only to a person to whom the offer was made. If the insurers impose higher rates than normal or more stringent terms after an offer by the proposer then it becomes a counter-offer which the proposer may accept or reject.

A1F Consensus ad idem

Unrevoked offer and unqualified acceptance are required. There must be complete agreement between the parties (a party may escape liability by showing that they were mistaken as to what has apparently been agreed, but mistake of law will not avoid the contract). There must be a 'meeting of minds'.

A1G Consideration

Where a person wishes to enforce a promise made to them by another then they must show that they gave something to, or did something for, that other person in return for the promise; for example, the premium is the consideration.

The consideration must 'move' from promisee to promisor; it need not be adequate but must be of some value and must be genuine. Consideration from the insured to the insurer is the premium. Consideration from the insurer to the insured is the promise to compensate the insured or to make certain payment in the event of certain events taking place. This promise is applicable whether or not a claim arises during the period of the insurance.

An easy way of remembering these seven essential elements is to think of the word 'COLPACC' which reminds us of capacity, offer, legality, possibility, acceptance, consensus and consideration.

A2 CONSTRUCTION OF CONTRACTS

The contract is construed according to ordinary language, except where terms are defined in a contract (for example, aviation and personal accident policies). The conditions of a contract are binding if agreed prior to completion.

A3 VALIDITY OF CONTRACTS

For a number of reasons a contract may not be fully valid in law. These contracts fall into the three following categories:

▶ void;
▶ voidable;
▶ unenforceable.

A3A Void

A ◆**void policy**◆ is a contract which is contrary to statute or public policy, or which is induced by fraud or when an essential element is missing. Such a contract cannot be enforced by either party.

A3B Voidable

A ◆**voidable policy**◆ is a policy which is open to one of the parties to avoid if they choose. The contract is 'valid until avoided'. A misrepresentation of material facts may give rise to this option (see utmost good faith, section B).

A3C Unenforceable

An unenforceable contract is one which fails because some evidential defect; for example, a marine insurance contract which has not been evidenced in writing. An unenforceable contract is valid in every respect, but it cannot be enforced in a court of law.

A4 TERMINATION OF CONTRACT

A contract may be terminated in the following ways:

▶ **Performance by all parties**. A contract is performed when each party has carried out his side of the bargain.

Performance by the insured primarily will involve payment of the agreed premium (although he may have additional duties under the terms of the policy). Performance by the insurers will involve bearing certain risks for an agreed period of time and paying any valid claims which arise.

If the period of insurance expires without any loss occurring, the insurers have nevertheless performed their part of the bargain by bearing the risk for the agreed term. However, the contract will not necessarily be discharged on the expiry date of the policy: in many cases, insurers will remain liable for losses sustained in the period of insurance even though they come to light and are reported some time afterwards.

▶ **Agreement between parties**. Since a contract is formed by agreement, it follows that the parties can make a further agreement to release each other from their obligations.

▶ **Frustration**. A contract may be terminated through subsequent impossibility (frustration).

The contract cannot be performed because after the time when the contract was made and prior to completion, an event occurs which destroys the basis of the contract but without the fault of either party.

A5 BREACH OF CONTRACT

Breach of contract is the failure to carry out obligations which does not terminate the contract but gives the other party a right of action for breach; for example, failure of insurers to pay a claim. The insured has a right of action against insurers which, in these circumstances, could be the award of damages.

A5A Remedies for breach

At common law, damages may be awarded which may be liquidated or unliquidated (the amount may be stated in the contract or not). The courts can also order specific performance (the contract must be performed) or grant an injunction (which is an order preventing an act).

B

UTMOST GOOD FAITH

♦**Utmost good faith**♦ is of vital importance in relation to insurance contracts. Let us now consider how the doctrine applies.

B1 NON-INSURANCE CONTRACTS

Most commercial contracts are subject to the doctrine of *caveat emptor* (let the buyer beware). Various Acts of Parliament protect the buyer in practice but each party is responsible for ensuring that they make a good deal.

B2 INSURANCE CONTRACTS

Q   In contrast to non-insurance contracts, insurance contracts put the proposer, in a sense, in a superior position. In what way do you think he holds a distinct advantage over the insurer?

A   Insurance contracts differ from commercial contracts because the proposer is the only person who knows all about the risk he wishes to insure and his own past insurance history.

Insurers have to rely on the information supplied by the proposer in their consideration of any risk.

The broker must ♦**disclose**♦ all facts disclosed by his client to him and any facts of which he is aware.

Insurers may ask questions as in a proposal form which the proposer must answer in full and truthfully; although for consumer insurances, insurers generally reduce this duty to the best of the proposer's knowledge and belief (see section B6, contractual duty). In certain cases their representatives may survey a risk. It is, therefore, necessary to have a principle which allows insurers to come off risk or refuse payment of a claim when an insurance has been obtained by telling untruths or hiding facts. There is a general duty of disclosure on the proposer in addition to answers given to any questions on the proposal form.

Similarly, insurers must clearly state the terms of the insurance clearly during negotiations.

The rule of utmost good faith applies in all insurance contracts and is a ♦**common law**♦ duty.

B3 MATERIAL FACTS

A duty is on the insured to state facts relating to a risk accurately. These are termed ♦**material facts**♦ and are those which would affect the acceptance or rating of a risk. This means that facts which would tend to make the risk of loss more likely or more severe must be disclosed to the insurer. Similarly, details of previous losses (whether insured or not), of special terms imposed by other insurers or of ♦**declinature**♦ must be disclosed.

B3A Duration of duty of utmost good faith

Q   What is the duration of the duty of utmost good faith?

A   This duty applies:

▶ throughout negotiation of a risk;

▶ to any alteration in the risk whilst that alteration is being negotiated with the insurers;

▶ to any renewal of the insurance.

B3B Facts which matter

Examples of facts which matter include the following:

▶ The refusal (declinature) of another insurer to renew an insurance policy of the type being negotiated.

▶ A firm omitting to state that one of the partners of the firm has been refused theft insurance whilst trading alone in the same goods on the same premises.

▶ A bungalow has a thatched roof rather than one of slates or tiles and therefore presents an increased fire risk.

B3C Facts which do not matter

Facts which fall into the following categories are not considered to be material facts and the proposer does not have a duty to disclose them to the insurer:

▶ facts which are totally irrelevant;

▶ facts which actually lessen the risk;

▶ facts which are public knowledge;

▶ facts which have already been disclosed in previous negotiations with the same insurer;

▶ facts which an insurer ought to know as a matter of professional competence;

▶ facts which are points of law.

B3D Alteration during policy period

A policy condition may require the insured to advise insurers of any increase or alteration in risk during the policy period. This is called the continuous duty of utmost good faith.

B3E Disclosure by broker

The broker is the agent for the insured and his responsibility is to his principal and jointly to see that insurers are fully informed of all material facts necessary to underwrite the risk.

B4 REPRESENTATIONS

◆**Representations**◆ are factual statements made verbally or in writing by the proposer or his broker which relate to the risk to be insured. They must be substantially true if they relate to matters of fact and, if they are not, insurers may refuse to pay a subsequent claim.

An example of a representation is as follows: 'No claims over the past fifteen years on a household policy'.

Thus a ◆**material representation**◆ is a statement made to the underwriter by the insured or his broker before acceptance of the risk which is material to his decision in accepting and rating the risk.

B5 BREACHES OF UTMOST GOOD FAITH

Breaches of utmost good faith may arise in one or both of the following ways:

▶ misrepresentation, which can be either innocent or fraudulent;

▶ non-disclosure, which can be either innocent or fraudulent. In the latter case it is usually termed 'concealment'.

◆**Non-disclosure**◆ is the omission to disclose a material fact inadvertently or because the proposer thought that it was immaterial. Concealment is the intentional suppression of a material fact.

Fraudulent ◆**misrepresentation**◆ is a statement made with the intention of deceiving the insurer, and known by the maker to be false, or made recklessly with no regard for truthfulness.

Innocent misrepresentation is an inaccurate statement relating to material facts which is really believed to be true by the person making it.

B5A Remedies of insurers

If the insured is in breach of utmost good faith then the policy may be of no effect from the time of the breach or insurers may refuse to pay a claim. Insurers may overlook the breach when they do not consider it to affect the risk or claim.

However, in the case of fraud, the policy has no legal validity.

B6 CONTRACTUAL DUTY

For consumer insurances the proposal form generally contains a declaration to be signed stating that, to the best of the insured's knowledge and belief, the information is true and agreeing that the proposal form is the basis of and is incorporated in the policy.

C

INSURABLE INTEREST

An insured can only take out an insurance policy if the happening of an insured event will cause him or his dependants financial or personal loss. This is termed ◆**insurable interest**◆, and is the legal right to insure, without which no insurance contract can be enforced in a court. Without the need for insurable interest, people could enter into gambling or wagering contracts which would be to the detriment of the other policyholders and the public as a whole. Anyone who has a legally recognised financial interest in what is insured is permitted to insure it.

C1 ESSENTIALS OF INSURABLE INTEREST

The three criteria that must exist if there is to be an insurable interest are as follows:

▶ There must be some property, interest, right, life or limb or potential liability which is capable of being insured.

▶ Such property, interest, right, life or limb or potential liability must be the subject matter of the insurance.

▶ The insured must stand in a relationship recognised by law to the subject matter of the insurance whereby he benefits from its safety or freedom from liabilities and is prejudiced by its loss, damage, delay, injury or creation of liability.

Example
Mr Smith cannot insure Mr Green's house because if the house is destroyed or damaged by fire then Mr Smith will not suffer any financial loss.

Similarly, Mr Smith cannot insure Mr Green's legal liability for accidents sustained by Mr Green's workmen, for if one of Mr Green's workmen should claim against his employer, Mr Green, then Mr Smith would not be financially concerned.

C2 PERSONS HAVING INSURABLE INTERESTS

? Can you think of examples of persons who may insure?

In answer to this question, the following are amongst those who may insure:

▶ Owners or joint owners of property with the permission of the other joint owner; for example, the joint owner can insure for the whole value of the property on behalf of the other building, plant, stock and so on.

- A person who has lawful possession of goods which belong to another: a dry cleaner, garage proprietor, ♦ **bailees of cargo** ♦ or hotel keeper.

- Those who have property within their care: an executor after someone's death.

- Agents: insurance brokers insuring on behalf of their clients.

- An underwriter: building societies may insure to the value of their loan.

- Anyone who may incur legal liabilities to others for negligent acts, or defects in property or goods.

C3 WHEN INSURABLE INTEREST MUST EXIST

In respect of non-marine policies, insurable interest must exist both when the policy is taken out and at the time of a claim. In respect of marine policies, insurable interest need only exist at the time of the claim. Marine policies differ because an interest may be acquired by the buyer of goods after the actual policy has been taken out by the original insured, i.e. the seller.

C3A Assignment

A non-marine policy cannot be transferred or assigned to a third party without the insurer's consent because the policy is regarded as a 'personal' contract between the insurer and the insured and rated partly on the record of the insured.

Marine cargo policies are normally freely assignable in accordance with the needs of maritime trade. The ♦ **assignment** ♦ of a marine hull policy needs agreement from the underwriters.

D

INDEMNITY

The object of an insurance policy is to place the insured in the same financial position as he was prior to any loss occurring. This principle applies to all insurance contracts, except those on life and of personal accident insurance where difficulties arise in placing values on life and limb. This principle is termed ♦ **indemnity** ♦.

Indemnity places the insured in the same financial position after a loss as that which existed prior to the loss happening. This principle is in accordance with the basic concept of insurance; namely, to compensate for misfortune but not to provide a profit from such misfortune.

D1 INDEMNITY IN PRACTICE

If a carpet was destroyed by a fire but at the time of the fire it was nearly worn out, it would be contrary to the principle of indemnity (and fairness to other policyholders) to pay the price of a new carpet. Otherwise, the insured would be tempted to destroy his own property. In this case, the insurers would pay the current price of a new carpet but would reduce the payment made to allow for the age and condition of the existing carpet.

Many household and commercial policies agree to replace items insured by new items provided the insured uses the value of new items in calculating the sum insured. This is termed '**new for old**' cover.

A liability policy provides indemnity to the insured in respect of his legal liability to pay damages plus claimant's and insured's costs and expenses. The policy does not, of course, define the amount which may be determined by a court of law, but it does state how indemnity will be calculated.

D1A Methods of indemnity

Indemnity may be provided by, for example:

- **cash payment**;

- **reinstatement**; for example, the cost of rebuilding a house paid by the insurers (this is rarely done due to the problems involved);

- **repair**; for example, repairs are authorised to a damaged motor vehicle and insurers pay the garage account;

► **replacement**; for example, when an aircraft is lost, insurers may replace it with an aircraft of similar age and type.

D1B Factors limiting the payment of indemnity

There are a number of factors which may restrict the insured to receiving less than a full indemnity in the event of a claim.

Where the insured and insurer agree in advance the amount to be paid in the event of total loss of property, then this is termed **valued policy**.

Where the insured bears part of the loss, termed an ◆**excess**◆, he will not be fully indemnified but may gain a reduction in premium for bearing an excess unless this has been imposed by the insurer.

An underwriter may impose an excess on an insured as a condition of acceptance of the risk. Similarly, young drivers may have a compulsory excess imposed.

In commercial insurances, excesses are often very large and the term 'deductible' is often preferred. A public liability policy may have a £25,000 deductible, meaning that the first £25,000 of any claim will be met by the insured. Marine policies on hulls normally contain a deductible for partial losses.

When the insured is under-insured he will not fully recover the actual true value in the event of a total loss and insurers may reduce partial losses payments by applying **pro rata average** where the insured is compelled to bear part of the loss himself.

Under a liability policy, average is not applied and the insured will only suffer if the award of damages together with costs exceeds the limit of indemnity, or any aggregate limit for any one year, shown in the policy.

E

SUBROGATION

The principle of ◆**subrogation**◆ is applicable only to contracts of indemnity. Once insurers have fully met the claim made, under common law they are entitled to take over all the legal rights of their insured so that the insurer's loss is cut down or fully recoverable.

Subrogation is a corollary of indemnity, in that an insured, who possesses rights under his policy and against third parties in respect of the same loss, would receive more than indemnity if he retained the proceeds of claims under both headings.

E1 HOW SUBROGATION MAY ARISE

Examples of how subrogation may arise include the following two instances:

► When an insured is involved in a motor accident caused by the negligence of another driver, insurers can seek to recover the damage to the insured vehicle from the other driver.

► Under the terms of a contract whereby a warehouseman is liable to pay part of any loss to the insured if the insured's goods are destroyed or damaged while in the warehouseman's possession.

Note: After paying for a total loss of property insurers may be entitled to the salvage remaining, i.e. the wreck of a car or damaged toys after a fire in a toy shop.

E2 MODIFICATIONS TO SUBROGATION

In practice, insurers can modify the common law position. Examples of such modifications are as follows:

► A policy condition in non-marine policies usually enables insurers to exercise their right of subrogation before payment of any claim is made to the insured by the insurers.

► Where legal liability is concerned, insurers often defend actions in court on behalf of their insured.

► Agreements, commonly called **knock for knock,** exist between insurers not to pursue rights of subrogation in motor insurance; each insurer paying for damage to the particular car he has insured.

▶ If an insured claims for damage to his vehicle from his insurers but also receives a payment from another motorist involved in the accident, he is expected to hold this payment in trust for insurers if he has already received payment from them.

▶ A further example is a 'third party sharing agreement' entered into between two motor insurers concerned with the settlement of claims for collision between two vehicles. However, details are beyond the scope of this book.

F
CONTRIBUTION

An insured may have more than one policy covering the same risk against the same peril. This may arise inadvertently (where an agent also insures property as well as a principal) or deliberately (where an insured doubts the security or cover of one policy). Under the rules of indemnity the insured is not allowed to claim more than the true amount of his loss. He should not claim the full loss from one insurer and a similar amount from other insurers.

F1 RIGHT OF CONTRIBUTION

♦**Contribution**♦ is the right of an insurer to call upon other insurers similarly, but not necessarily equally, liable to the same insured to share the cost of an indemnity payment. Thus contribution only arises under contracts of indemnity.

The principle of contribution allows the insured to claim the full loss from one insurer who then has the right to ask the other insurers who are also liable to share the claims payment. At common law, rights arise **after** a loss has been paid to the insured and insurers then have to share the loss between themselves.

F1A Policy condition

The principle of contribution is often modified by a policy condition since most non-marine policies contain a clause limiting insurers' liability to their share of the loss when other policies also exist. Thus, the insured is obliged to claim proportionately from each insurer.

An example in respect of property insurance is as follows:

$$\frac{\textbf{Sum insured by individual insurer x loss}}{\textbf{Total sum insured}}$$

F1B Non-contribution clause

Some policies contain a clause which states that the loss will not be shared if the property is listed separately in another policy. This is termed the **non-contribution clause**.

For example, a home policy on contents would not cover specified items of jewellery insured separately under a jewellery, furs and personal effects policy.

G
PROXIMATE CAUSE

When a claim is presented to underwriters or their representatives they will have regard to the doctrine of ♦**proximate cause**♦; that is, how exactly did the loss occur? Every loss is the effect of some cause and some insurance policies cover either a limited list of causes (as in the fire policy) or a wide range of causes (as in the 'all risks' type of policy): it is essential that the cause of any one loss is examined carefully. There may be a single cause or a chain of causes, one prompted by the other.

However a loss may occur, it is essential that the cause is one which falls within the scope of the policy for the underwriters to be held liable under the policy.

G1 CAUSE OF LOSSES

There is a valid claim under a policy of insurance only if the loss, damage or liability arises from an insured peril. Thus, when a claim occurs, the cause of the loss must be established to decide whether or not it is within the cover of the policy.

At law, only the dominant and effective cause of the loss is considered. Any other remote causes are disregarded. The cause of a loss may be an insured peril specifically mentioned in the policy or a peril specifically excluded by the policy or a cause which the policy does not mention. The law states that the sequence of events leading from the insured peril to the actual loss must be unbroken for the loss to be payable under the policy. Thus, circumstances can arise when an excluded peril is the genuine cause of the loss and insurers are not therefore liable for the loss.

G2 HOW PROXIMATE CAUSE IS APPLIED

When there is only one cause, like a fire, an explosion or a theft, then the problem is only one of determining whether or not the cause was insured.

Where there is a single cause which is an insured peril (for example, fire under a fire policy) then the insurers are liable. Where there is an excluded cause followed by an insured peril if no break occurs (for example, riot causing a fire) then the insurers are not liable. Where an uninsured peril (i.e. one not mentioned in the policy) caused the loss then the insurers are not liable. At all times the onus of proof that a loss is caused by an insured peril rests upon the claimant.

The courts and insurers always consider the dominant cause of a loss which need not necessarily be the cause nearest in point of time but is one which 'the man in the street' would consider the nearest and most efficient cause.

G3 PROXIMATE CAUSE IN PRACTICE

An example of how proximate cause is applied in practice would be in the following situation: if a vessel is torpedoed and damaged but sinks during a subsequent storm, insurers will not consider that the storm caused the sinking (although nearest in point of time) but that the torpedo was the real cause of the loss.

The principle operates to benefit both insurer and insured as follows:

▶ the **insurer** is secure from claims for losses remotely caused by a peril insured against but effectively caused by a peril outside the scope of the policy;

▶ the **insured** is protected against non-payment of a reasonable claim although a remote cause is not a peril insured against.

H

WARRANTIES

When an underwriter writes a risk, how can he be sure that the facts are as stated by the insured via his broker and that the risk will not become more hazardous by the insured's conduct? Insurers may include in an insurance policy a stipulation which should be complied with by the insured. These are termed ◆**warranties**◆ and are used to control the nature of a risk.

A warranty is an undertaking as to fact or performance concerning the risk written into an insurance policy and may need to be complied with strictly and literally.

The MIA 1906 defines a warranty as something:

... by which the assured undertakes that some particular thing shall or shall not be done, or that some condition shall be fulfilled, or whereby he affirms or negatives the existence of a particular state of facts.

H1 BREACH OF WARRANTY

Non-compliance constitutes breach of warranty and the insurer is discharged from liability as from the date of breach. However, the Statement of General Insurance Practice, which does not apply to marine and aviation risks and only applies to policyholders resident in the UK and insured in their private capacity, states that insurers will not repudiate liability to indemnify a policyholder on the grounds of a breach of warranty or condition where the circumstances of the loss are unconnected with the breach unless fraud is involved. The statement has been voluntarily adopted by all Lloyd's underwriters.

H2 EXPRESS WARRANTIES

Examples of express warranties include the following:

Fire insurance warranties:

► that all oily or greasy rags be placed in metal receptacles and removed from the building daily;

► that not more than 200 gallons of paraffin be kept in an ironmonger's premises at any one time.

Burglary insurance warranties:

► that premises are not unoccupied at night;
► that certain types of approved locks are fitted.

Marine insurance warranty:

► that goods are packed in tin-lined cases.

Non-compliance with a warranty may be excused by insurers if they are notified and an additional premium paid if required.

H3 IMPLIED WARRANTIES

Implied warranties are found only in marine insurance and are warranties which are automatically applicable, although they do not appear in the policy document. An example of an implied warranty is a statement that a vessel is seaworthy.

SUMMARY

A number of important features relating to legal principles have been described in this chapter. In fact we have only introduced some principles which are complex in practice. In the next chapter we will look at one further legal principle, that of the law of agency.

4
GLOSSARY OF TERMS

Assignment
The passing of beneficial rights from one party to another. A policy or certificate of insurance cannot be assigned after interest has passed, unless an agreement to assign was made, or implied, prior to the passing of interest. An assignee acquires no greater rights than were held by the assignor, and a breach of good faith by the assignor is deemed to be a breach on the part of the assignee.

Bailees of cargo
Persons in temporary possession of cargo that is the property of another; for example, carriers, warehouse keepers.

Common law
The law which has been founded upon immemorial usage, established custom and legal decisions, as distinct from statute law.

Contribution
The division of a loss between insurers where two or more cover the same insured, the same risk and the same interests; for example so as to cause over-insurance by double insurance. Contribution arises from the principle of indemnity and ensures equitable distribution of losses between insurers.

Declinature
Refusal of an insurer to accept or renew a proposal for insurance.

Disclosure
The duty of the insured and his broker to tell the underwriter every material fact before acceptance of the risk.

Excess
The first portion of a loss, being an agreed percentage or fixed sum, which the insured agrees to bear or a portion another insurer is bearing.

Indemnity
Indemnity is the legal principle which ensures that a policyholder is restored to the same financial position after the loss as he was in immediately prior to the loss.

Insurable interest
The insured's financial interest in the subject matter of the insurance. A policy where the insured is without such interest is unenforceable.

Insurance contract
An agreement between an insurer and one or more parties, called the insured, whereby the insurer undertakes in return for the payment of a consideration, called the premium, to pay to the insured a sum of money or to grant certain compensation on the happening of a specified event.

Material facts
Any fact or circumstance which would affect the judgment of a prudent underwriter in considering whether he would accept the risk or not and at which rate of premium.

Material representation
A statement made to the underwriter before acceptance of risk, which is material to his decision in accepting and rating the risk.

Misrepresentation
A mis-statement of fact made by the insured or his broker to the underwriter, before acceptance of the risk, which misleads the underwriter in assessing the risk and induces the contract. If the representation is material and amounts to misrepresentation, it is a breach of utmost good faith.

Non-disclosure
Failure by the insured or his broker to disclose a material fact or circumstance to the underwriter before acceptance of the risk.

Proximate cause
The active, efficient cause which sets in motion a train of events which brings about a result without the intervention of any new cause working actively from a fresh or independent source. Proximate cause is thus not necessarily the closest in time to the result.

Representation
A statement of fact made by the insured or his broker when negotiating an insurance with the underwriter.

Subrogation
The right of the underwriter to take over the insured's rights following payment of a claim to recover the payment from a third party responsible for the loss. Limited to the amount paid on the policy.

Utmost good faith (*uberrima fides*)
A contract of insurance is a contract based upon the utmost good faith, and if the utmost good faith is breached by either party then the contract may be avoided by the other party.

Void policy
One which does not exist.

Voidable policy
Where the underwriter or insured has the right to avoid a policy (for example, in the event of a breach of utmost good faith) the policy is termed 'voidable'.

Warranty
It is defined as a 'warranty by which the insured undertakes that some particular thing shall or shall not be done, or that some condition shall be fulfilled, or whether he affirms or negates the existence of a particular state of facts'. Non-compliance constitutes breach of warranty and the underwriter is discharged from liability as from the date of the breach.

4

MULTIPLE CHOICE QUESTIONS

1.   A contract may be terminated in three of the following ways. Which answer is incorrect?

   (a)   ✓Performance by all parties.
   (b)   By agreement between the parties.
   (c)   By breach.   ☑ ✓
   (d)   By frustration or subsequent impossibility.

2.   Some insurance contracts have, by law, to be evidenced in writing. To which of the following contracts does this apply?

   (a)   All airport liability policies.
   (b)   All marine hull and cargo insurance policies.   ☑ ✓
   (c)   All livestock insurance policies involving imported animals.
   (d)   Any insurance contract with foreign nationals.

3.   Which of the following statements is incorrect?

   The duty of utmost good faith applies:

   (a)   throughout the negotiation of a risk;
   (b)   only to the insured;   ☑ ✓
   (c)   during any renewal of the insurance;
   (d)   while any alteration to the risk is being arranged.

4.   Which of the following statements is correct?

   (a)   Disclosure is solely the duty of the insured.
   (b)   The disclosure of material facts has to be obtained by skilful questioning on the part of the insurer.
   (c)   Disclosure is simply the answering of all the questions on the proposal form.   ✓
   (d)   Disclosure is the duty of the insured, his broker and the insurer.   ☑

5. What is the meaning of *uberrima fides?*

    (a) Unlimited liability.
    (b) Maximum security.
    (c) Utmost good faith.
    (d) Attractive conditions.

6. 'A material fact is one which would affect the judgment of a prudent underwriter when considering whether to enter into a contract at one rate of premium or another, or not at all. A material fact includes any comunication made to the proposer or any information received by him'.

    Non-disclosure, concealment or misrepresentation of a material fact may render an insurance policy voidable at the election of the aggrieved party.

    Having regard to the above, which of the following is correct in the case of an insurance contract?

    (a) Material facts include those which are matters of opinion.
    (b) Material facts which are public knowledge, for example, state of war, must be disclosed.
    (c) Disclosure is required of facts which lessen a risk; for example, alarm systems fitted.
    (d) Disclosure of a material fact is a positive duty.

7. A representation is a statement made during insurance contract negotiations. Which one of the following statements applies?

    (a) All representations are material and must be correct.
    (b) Those representations which are material must be substantially true.
    (c) Those representations which are material must be totally correct.
    (d) Any misrepresentation will allow insurers to sue for damages.

8. When does insurable interest first arise?

    (a) At the inception of a policy.
    (b) On receipt of a quotation for a policy.
    (c) When subjected to the risk of a loss or certain liability.
    (d) When an accident is due to another party's negligence.

MULTIPLE CHOICE QUESTIONS

9. Which one of the following people do not have an insurable interest?

    (a) A garage owner who has possession of any other person's car which happens to be in his garage for repair. ☐

    (b) A man who wishes to back a certain horse in the Grand National and insures himself against injury to the horse in the week prior to the race. ☑

    (c) An underwriter who wishes to insure himself against having to pay out too much in claims made by people he has insured. ☐

    (d) A business partner wishing to insure a building which he jointly owns with other partners. ☐

10. In which of the following cases does contribution apply?

    (a) When more than one insurer covers a risk. ☑
    (b) When premiums are paid by instalments. ☐
    (c) When the insured property has joint owners. ☐
    (d) When the insured property has been under-valued. ☐

11. 'The placing of the insured in the same position after a loss as immediately before the happening of an insured event, in so far as this is possible.'

    What principle does the above describe?

    (a) Subrogation. ☐
    (b) Security. ☐
    (c) Rectification. ☐
    (d) Indemnity. ☑

12. Which of the following describes the right granted to insurers by the doctrine of subrogation?

    (a) To take over and handle any claim made against the insured. ☐

    (b) To take advantage of every right of the insured in attempting to recover an outlay made to indemnify the insured. ☑

    (c) To deal only with their own insured's claim and not seek recovery from any negligent third party's insurers. ☐

    (d) To take over salvage, including any profit. ☐

4

ANSWERS TO MULTIPLE CHOICE QUESTIONS

1. Answer (c), breach.

2. Answer (b), all marine hull and cargo contracts have to be evidenced in writing in order to be legally enforceable.

3. Answer (b), only to the insured.

4. Answer (d), disclosure is the duty of all parties.

5. Answer (c), utmost good faith.

6. Answer (d), disclosure of a material fact is a positive duty.

7. Answer (b), representations which are material must be substantially true.

8. Answer (c), when subjected to the risk of a loss or certain liability.

9. Answer (b), the gambler does not have an insurable interest.

10. Answer (a), when more than one insurer covers a risk.

11. Answer (d), indemnity.

12. Answer (b), to take advantage of every right of the insured in attempting to recover an outlay made to indemnify the insured.

5

AGENCY; LLOYD'S BROKERS

A Agency

B Duties and responsibilities of a broker

INTRODUCTION

In this chapter we will examine the simple basis of the law of agency, mention briefly Lloyd's underwriting agents (which will be dealt with in more depth in chapter 7) and examine the duties and responsibilities of a broker and, more particularly, a Lloyd's broker.

Insurance brokers have been an established feature of Lloyd's from the early days when Lloyd's was still a coffee house where merchants met to discuss their business ventures. The part played by brokers was an essential one since, frequently, the underwriters were full-time professionals in other fields who had the means but neither the time nor the inclination to seek out risks for themselves to insure, and no single underwriter would be prepared to risk too much on any one vessel or cargo.

Thus, brokers went to likely insurers who met at Lloyd's, each of whom would hopefully 'write a line' under the leading name on the broker's slip until he had 100% cover for the risk in question. The role of the broker has evolved along with the business of insurance at Lloyd's.

LEARNING OBJECTIVES

After studying this chapter, you should be able to:

▷ outline the basic features of the law of agency;

▷ illustrate a broker's responsibilities to the client and underwriter;

▷ identify and discuss the duties and responsibilities of Lloyd's brokers, particularly their duty of utmost good faith.

A

AGENCY

An ♦**agent**♦ is a person who is employed to do something in the place of another, and the person who employs him is called the **principal**.

The law of agency is based on the maxim 'he who employs another to do something is deemed to have done it himself'. Any person who has contractual capacity may employ an agent and, if he does so, is (subject to various qualifications, which are beyond the scope of this book) bound by what the agent does on his behalf.

A1 APPOINTMENT OF AGENTS

Insurance brokers are the agent of the insured, although in practice or by custom they may also accept such appointments or responsibilities from others.

The appointment of an agent may be by:

▶ an agreement in writing (i.e. by express agreement);
▶ implication or conduct or by the situation of the parties;
▶ necessity;
▶ imposition.

In turn, agents may be:

▶ special (for a specific act only);
▶ general (empowered to do anything within certain limits);
▶ universal (unlimited powers).

In practical terms, this means the following:

▶ **By express agreement**. Either verbally or in writing a specific appointment will be made which may contain conditions; for example, a letter of appointment by a client or an insurance company's agency agreement.

▶ **By implication or conduct**. Someone may permit another to obtain or do things for him and commonly approve of what is done. For example, a client may accept renewals automatically made on his behalf. Thus the agency is inferred from the conduct of the parties, or is implied by law.

▶ **By necessity**. It may be impossible to get a principal's instructions, and a necessity arises forcing an agent to deal with the events; for example, preserving property in an emergency.

A principal is bound by any act which the agent does within the scope of his authority. He is also bound, however, if he ratifies (that is, adopts as his own act) an act which the agent has done without authority.

If an agent does not have authority to contract for his principal or has exceeded his powers, then there is no binding contract. It may be possible for the agent to obtain ratification of his acts without authority later. However, if this is not possible then a personal responsibility may well remain in the absence of some defence being available.

A2 TERMINATION OF AGENCY

Should it be wished to terminate the relationship between a principal and an agent then this may be accomplished by mutual agreement, revocation or operation of the law.

A mutual agreement to end a relationship should nevertheless deal with all aspects of the severance. There is no set procedure, but an exchange of letters or a record of conversations is important to avoid future liabilities being imposed on the agent. This record of events should indicate the date of termination, how the disposal of information and documents will be carried out, what responsibilities remain and how unpaid debts will be met.

The general rule is that the principal may revoke the authority which he has given to his agent at any time, and the agency will thus come to an end.

However, where a principal has allowed third parties to deal with an agent, and later revokes the agent's authority, he is liable in respect of contracts made by the agent with third parties if the latter had no choice of the revocation.

Operation of the law may terminate agency relationships where:

▶ the period of appointment has expired;

▶ a particular transaction for which the agent was appointed has been completed or an agreed event has taken place;

▶ the agency has become unlawful;

▶ there has been death or insanity;

▶ there has been bankruptcy or liquidation.

A3 LLOYD'S UNDERWRITING AGENTS

Lloyd's functions by the members delegating all underwriting and claim-settling authority to ◆**underwriting agents**◆.

When Lloyd's was smaller, few formal agreements were formed between members and their agents. As Lloyd's grew, the need for standard formal agency contracts became apparent. As members have unlimited liability they could be considered particularly vulnerable.

The regulatory framework has been devised partly in order to:

▶ recognise the pivotal role of the underwriting agents;

▶ maintain confidence and trust between the member and his agent;

▶ establish standards for agents.

Lloyd's underwriting agency agreements are now expressly detailed so as to reduce any potential for doubt.

B

DUTIES AND RESPONSIBILITIES OF A BROKER

In general terms, the broker may be described as an intermediary who stands between the supplier of a service (in this case, the Lloyd's underwriter or the insurance company) and the individual who wishes to acquire that service (the client or proposer, who will become the insured or reinsured). The broker's presence in this chain to some extent simplifies the flow of business to the insurer, and relieves the proposer of the need to communicate with different syndicates or companies involved in his risk. The broker is the channel of communication with the expertise necessary to minimise misunderstandings between the two parties and to pave the way to a contract agreeable to both sides.

B1 FUNCTIONS OF A BROKER

The functions of a broker are three-fold, namely to:

▶ act as an intermediary;
▶ be a professional adviser;
▶ represent his client's interests.

B2 INSURANCE BROKERS

The **EEC Intermediaries Directive (1976)** defines an insurance broker as follows:

Professional activities of persons who, acting with complete freedom as to their choice of undertaking, bring together, with a view to the insurance or reinsurance of risks, persons seeking insurance or reinsurance and insuranceor reinsurance undertakings, carry out work preparatory to the conclusion of contracts of insurance or reinsurance and, where appropriate, assist in the administration and performance of such contracts, in particular in the event of a claim.

The prime difference between insurance agents and insurance brokers is that an agent answers directly to the insurer; the insurance broker relates to the policyholder. To this extent, therefore, the term 'agent' has come to have a special meaning beyond the simple agent dealt within the law agency.

A broker is an individual or firm whose full-time occupation is the placing of insurance with insurers. Legislation exists which governs the use of the word 'broker'.

The insured can obtain independent advice on a wide range of insurance matters from a broker, without direct cost to himself. The broker will advise on insurance needs, best type of cover and its restrictions, best market, claims procedure, obligations placed on the insurance by policy conditions, and he will update the information to take account of market changes.

B3   DUTIES OF A BROKER

The general law of agency requires that an insurance broker assumes responsibilities which require him to:

▶ exercise due diligence in carrying out instructions within the responsibilities which he has undertaken;

▶ exercise any skill he professes to have;

▶ ensure that the client is aware of factors likely to affect his judgment in fulfilment of the contract;

▶ render an account and not make any secret commission or profit beyond normal remuneration;

▶ maintain confidentiality; and

▶ only delegate authority with specific permission.

B4   INSURANCE BROKER AND RESPONSIBILITY FOR NEGLIGENCE

An insurance broker, like any other professional, is legally responsible to his principal or other in the event that he fails to use reasonable care.

The duties of care exercised are high and this was emphasised in the case of **Hedley Byrne v. Heller (1963)** where it was held that care on advice given had to be exercised by persons even without any formal contract. An insurance broker must be certain of the advice he gives in addition to carrying out specific and required acts on behalf of his principal.

B5   RIGHTS OF AN INSURANCE BROKER

The insurance broker has a right of support from his principal in carrying out his responsibilities as agent of the insured. It is the duty of the principal to indemnify his agent for acts lawfully done and liabilities incurred in the carrying out of the responsibilities involved.

The right to the commission earned is fundamental and the fact that, physically, the commission is paid by the insurer by deduction does not make the broker the agent of the insurer.

B6   BROKER'S RESPONSIBILITY

In connection with the transaction of business involving Lloyd's underwriters, it is the long-standing custom that a Lloyd's broker is liable to the underwriters for the premium. So far as marine insurance is concerned, this custom has been embodied in the MIA 1906 S.53(i). It must be emphasised that the practice applies to all business placed at Lloyd's, not only marine insurance.

B7   UTMOST GOOD FAITH

The broker is the agent for the insured and not only must he disclose what has been communicated to him by his principal, but he must also disclose any circumstance of which he himself (though not the principal) may have knowledge.

B8   BROKER'S RESPONSIBILITY TO HIS CLIENT

A broker's first responsibility is to his client. He will interpret his client's wishes and, when necessary, clarify these, resulting in a proposal from the client which will translate into an offer to an underwriter.

At all times he will advance his client's interests and obtain the best possible terms and conditions. He will also endeavour to achieve the lowest possible premium commensurate with the security of the market he approaches.

On completion of placing the risk, the broker will advise his client and produce a cover note confirming the agreed terms and conditions and setting out the security, i.e. the list of underwriters subscribing to the risk.

The broker thereafter will give the client the service he can reasonably expect, with particular reference to the accounting of monies, both premiums and claims.

B9 BROKER'S RESPONSIBILITY TO THE UNDERWRITER

A broker's responsibility to the underwriter is essentially a **duty of care**; that is to say, any undertaking given to the underwriter must be honoured and no material information withheld. Whilst the broker must portray the client proposal in the most favourable light, this must not be at the expense of an honest presentation or, at worst, result in a mischievous or even fraudulent misrepresentation.

The broker must, therefore, present to the underwriter all the information at his disposal which is needed by the underwriter to make a fair and reasonable appreciation of the risk being offered. After the risk has been placed and any short-signing commitment has been honoured, the broker will continue to have a responsibility to the underwriter as far as monetary transactions are concerned.

The broker will pay the premiums (which he has collected from his client) to the underwriters within a reasonable time and within the period laid down at the time of placing the risk.

Should claims become payable, the details must be shown by the broker to the underwriter in an honest way as advised by the client. Likewise, the monies, once collected, must be transmitted promptly to the client to avoid any further distress being suffered by the claimant and put to the underwriters in a favourable light in the eye of the insured.

B10 THE LLOYD'S BROKER

Firms of ♦**Lloyd's brokers**♦ operate under the provisions of the **Lloyd's Brokers Bye-law (No.5 of 1988)** and the code of practice for Lloyd's brokers and, as we have seen, are committed to additional responsibilities on behalf of Lloyd's underwriters beyond normal insurance broking practice and within the general law of agency.

Wherever a Lloyd's broking firm is conducting business, its responsibilities will be considerable, whether they arise through presenting the risk or conducting negotiations for claims settlement.

Such additional responsibilities include the preparation of policies which are submitted to **Lloyd's Policy Signing Office (LPSO)** for checking and signature on behalf of underwriters. Accounting between Lloyd's brokers and underwriters is transacted under the central accounting scheme which inevitably necessitates the application of procedures which vary the broker's position in law by comparison with their dealings with insurance companies.

B10A Lloyd's broker's responsibilities

At this stage it is worth looking in more detail at the responsibilities of a Lloyd's broker:

Defining the client's insurance requirements
Like any broker, a Lloyd's broker's first task will be to ascertain the client's insurance requirements. The broker should bear in mind not only the options available and the information needed before approaching an underwriter, but also the proportion of the risk that the broking firm is being asked to place and the likely cost. The broker should also take account of the client's experience, or possible inexperience, in assessing what type of cover he requires.

Obtaining quotes for the client/utmost good faith
The Lloyd's broker may approach insurers in the Lloyd's or company markets depending on where its client is likely to be best served. If the firm's placing broker chooses the Lloyd's market then he will need firstly to identify an underwriter willing to lead.

The broker must approach one or, ideally, a number of possible 'leaders' for quotations on the terms of cover they will provide and at what cost. This will involve the preparation of a slip and certainly will require the provision of some supplementary information relating to the risk to fulfil the duty of disclosure of all material facts. If a broker suspects a client of withholding information about a risk, then the broker should have regard to his own duty of utmost good faith and refuse to place the risk.

Accepting a quote and placing the risk
Having, where necessary, assisted the client in accepting a quote, the broker places the risk and

completes the cover. The broking firm will prepare a placing slip giving details of the risk.

Informing the client

It is then the broker's duty to inform his client of the nature of the contract that has been agreed, particularly the date upon which cover began. The broker may do this orally but will confirm, in writing, in the form of a cover note which will include the principal details of the insurance. The broker may issue a debit note at this stage for the amount of premium due or otherwise at the time of the preparation of the client's accounts.

Collection of premiums

The broking firm organises a system to collect the premiums due from clients. It will need to check the accuracy of commission deducted by any other intermediaries operating between itself and the original client. The broker will then deduct his own brokerage and pay the remaining 'net absolute premium' to the underwriter.

Payment of premiums to underwriters

With the exception of amounts due to motor syndicates, premiums for Lloyd's underwriters are paid by brokers via Lloyd's central settlement.

Preparing policies for signing by LPSO on behalf of underwriters

The policy constitutes written evidence of the contract between the insurer and the policyholder. The broker prepares the policy in accordance with details on the slip, and submits both (together with the London premium advice note, unless the premium has already been paid to underwriters) to the LPSO for checking.

Issuing policies to clients or holding those policies on the client's behalf

When LPSO has checked, signed and embossed the policy it will return it to the broker, attaching a signing schedule to identify the syndicates involved in the insurance and their respective participations. It is then the broker's responsibility to send the policy to the client or to retain it on the client's behalf if so arranged.

Endorsements

This is an adjustment made to the cover, whether a supplement to or extension of its terms. The broking firm will have the changes to the cover agreed and will submit the endorsement wording to the LPSO for checking and signing, any amounts of additional premium being processed in the usual way.

Renewals

A broker may be able to renew an insurance by approaching the underwriters who subscribed to the expiring policy. Where some of these wish to withdraw, the broker may have to approach further insurers, or continuing underwriters may agree to take larger lines. The broker may also approach other insurers for alternative quotations.

Inwards and outwards reinsurances

▶ **Inwards reinsurance:** the procedures described above apply equally whether the broker is placing insurance or reinsurance business.

▶ **Syndicate reinsurance:** the Lloyd's broker may be requested to arrange ◆**outwards reinsurance**◆, for a Lloyd's underwriter wishing to reinsure his own syndicate.

Claims

When the client wishes to make a claim on his insurance, he turns to the broker to advise the insurers involved and to collect the claims monies. The broker will either credit the client's account or pay the claim amount directly to him.

SUMMARY

We have concluded our look at legal principles and have examined in practical terms the duties and responsibilities of Lloyd's brokers to underwriters and to their clients.

Brokers are an essential feature of Lloyd's, with a history dating back almost as far as that of the underwriters themselves. They bring the vital business to the underwriters and provide a professional service to the market, guiding their clients through the maze of complexities that may confront them.

In the next chapter we will consider the market at Lloyd's, commencing with a brief review of the history of the society.

5

GLOSSARY OF TERMS

Agent

A person empowered to act on behalf of another.

Lloyd's broker

A partnership or corporate body permitted by the Council to broke insurance business at Lloyd's.

Outwards reinsurance

The reinsurance of Lloyd's syndicates.

Underwriting agent

A registered underwriting agent is a firm or company permitted by the Council to act as an underwriting agency at Lloyd's.

5

MULTIPLE CHOICE QUESTIONS

1. Which of these statements is incorrect?

   An agent may be appointed:

   (a) by an agreement in writing;
   (b) posthumously;
   (c) by implication or conduct;
   (d) by necessity.

2. Which of the following is incorrect?

   An agent may be:

   (a) special;
   (b) conditional;
   (c) general;
   (d) universal.

3. Which of the following is not a function of a broker?

   (a) To pay an insured's claim if an underwriter defaults.
   (b) To be a professional adviser.
   (c) To represent his client's interests.
   (d) To act as an intermediary.

4. Which of the following statements is incorrect?

   A broker:

   (a) must not make any commission or profit beyond normal remuneration;
   (b) may delegate his authority as necessary, without the need to confirm this action with his principal;
   (c) must not discuss his client's business with other clients;
   (d) is required to exercise whatever skills he professes to have.

5

MULTIPLE CHOICE QUESTIONS

5.   A broker's first responsibility is to:

    (a)   the Council of Lloyd's;

    (b)   his client; ☑

    (c)   Lloyd's Insurance Brokers' Committee;

    (d)   the underwriter.

6.   When placing business, a broker is acting for:

    (a)   his principal; ☑

    (b)   the insurer;

    (c)   both the insured and underwriters;

    (d)   his agent.

7.   Which one of the following statements is correct?

    (a)   An insurance agent is directly responsible to the insured.

    (b)   An insurance agent is directly responsible to the broker.

    (c)   An insurance broker is directly responsible to the insured. ☑

    (d)   An insurance broker is directly responsible to the insurer.

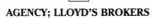
ANSWERS TO SELF-ASSESSMENT QUESTIONS APPEAR OVERLEAF

5

ANSWERS TO MULTIPLE CHOICE QUESTIONS

1.   Answer (b), posthumously, is incorrect.

2.   Answer (b), conditional, is incorrect.

3.   Answer (a), is not a function of a broker.

4.   Answer (b) is incorrect.

5.   Answer (b), his client.

6.   Answer (a), his principal.

7.   Answer (c), an insurance broker is directly responsible to the insured.

HISTORY OF LLOYD'S AND THE LLOYD'S MARKET

A   History of Lloyd's

B   The Lloyd's market

INTRODUCTION

In any field of study a knowledge of the origins of the subject is useful. This is particularly so of insurance and the Lloyd's market where the present makes more sense if we have an understanding of the development of Lloyd's over the past 300 years. In this chapter we will examine Lloyd's as a Society and a market, and the organisation of the market.

Insurances are placed **at** Lloyd's with syndicates representing members of the Society, rather than with the Corporation of Lloyd's itself.

A

HISTORY OF LLOYD'S

In the seventeenth century, insurance of ships and cargoes was often underwritten by merchants who were willing to carry part of the risk of a voyage in return for part of the premium. Commerce of various types was transacted among the merchants who met each other at various coffee houses around the City of London. Similarly, those wishing to transact insurance would meet in these coffee houses. One of them, owned by Edward Lloyd, was situated near the River Thames and was frequented by merchants, shipowners and others having an interest in maritime ventures.

A1   THE GROWTH OF LLOYD'S AND LLOYD'S REGULATIONS

Lloyd's Coffee House was situated in Tower Street and was in existence by 1688, although the original date of opening is uncertain. Edward Lloyd encouraged the merchants, or 'underwriters' (they signed their names at the foot of the insurance contracts), because it brought extra business to his coffee house. He supplied shipping information and published a news sheet in 1696, called 'Lloyd's News'. This was superseded some years after his death by '**Lloyd's List**', which is London's oldest newspaper.

In 1720, the London Assurance and the Royal Exchange were granted Royal Charters to transact marine insurance. The Act providing for the incorporation of two companies restricted the provision of marine insurance to these two companies or to individuals. Lloyd's Coffee House prospered and Lloyd's had developed as a market place for insurance provided by individuals. The monopoly was eventually terminated in 1824.

In 1769, the insurance market transferred its business centre to the New Lloyd's Coffee House in Pope's Head Alley, and in 1771 a committee was formed to seek larger premises. With their membership subscriptions, premises were established in 1774 in the Royal Exchange. The formation of the Committee took the running of Lloyd's out of the hands of the coffee house owner and into the hands of the insurance fraternity.

The first deposit was made voluntarily with the Committee of Lloyd's in 1857 by an underwriting member.

The **Lloyd's Act 1871** made Lloyd's for the first time an incorporated society, with a written constitution and the power to make bye-laws. From 1882 all new entrants had to put up a deposit or guarantee (previously any such deposit or guarantee had been purely at the Committee's discretion). Although the **Lloyd's Act 1871** only referred to 'the carrying on of marine insurance business by members', Lloyd's increasingly was engaging in non-marine business, starting with home fire insurance. The **Lloyd's Act 1911** amended the 1871 Act to 'the carrying on by members of the Society of the business of insurance of every description...'.

that all underwriting members' accounts should be audited by an approved auditor with a view to certifying solvency and that all premiums, not just those received by new members, should be paid into a trust fund.

It was fortunate for Lloyd's that these measures were agreed in 1908 for in the following year Parliament passed the **Assurance Companies Act 1909** to regulate fire and accident insurance. The Committee, thanks to the new system of audit, gained for Lloyd's underwriters important exemptions from the provisions of this Act. The Act made both the audit and premium trust fund compulsory.

The Lloyd's Act of 1871 has been followed by five further Acts to meet the Society's changing needs. The most recent of these, **Lloyd's Act 1982**, resulted from the report of a working party which examined the Society's constitution and the effectiveness of its powers of self-regulation. The working party, established by Lloyd's in 1979 and chaired by a former High Court judge, Sir Henry Fisher, recommended the formation of a new body, the Council of Lloyd's, to assume the rule-making and disciplinary functions hitherto vested in Lloyd's membership as a whole.

A Bill to give effect to this and other changes was overwhelmingly endorsed by the membership in November 1980 and enacted in July 1982 after lengthy debate and detailed scrutiny by committees of both Houses of Parliament.

A1B Membership

Until 1968, membership was only open to male British Commonwealth nationals. Nationals of countries outside the British Commonwealth were admitted in 1968, women domiciled in the UK were admitted in 1969 and women of any nationality were admitted in 1970.

A1A Statutory control

In 1903 the Committee of Lloyd's made a first step to regulate the conduct of underwriting members by asking new members to agree to put their premiums in trust for the payment of underwriting liabilities. However, more far-reaching steps to tighten security were taken in 1908, when a general meeting agreed

A1C Development of direct business

Turning now to the development of direct insurance business (we have already considered marine risks), the initial expansion of the non-marine market is largely due to Cuthbert Heath's efforts during the 1880s when he wrote the first burglary risks and the first loss of profits fire contracts.

1911

The first aviation risk was written in the Lloyd's market as early as 1991. Motor risks were written by Lloyd's underwriters as the motor car developed, the first policy being the 'Red Cross' motor policy at Lloyd's in 1907.

A1D Development of reinsurance at Lloyd's

There is no clear record of the early involvement of Lloyd's in the acceptance of reinsurance. Lloyd's underwriters had usually each accepted the line appropriate for himself, with the broker spreading the risk through the market. The earliest record is a fire reinsurance treaty accepted by Heath in 1883. This was followed by his acceptance of the first American non-marine risk for an English company writing business in the United States of America in 1898.

The development of reinsurance was steady, with marine reinsurance being accepted on a considerable scale. Many new forms of insurance provided an obvious opportunity for underwriters to accept such reinsurances, and brokers increasingly produced business from overseas, particularly the United States. Finally, the development of excess of loss reinsurance from 1907 was an avenue naturally adapted for the enterprise of Lloyd's underwriters, so that today reinsurance represents a very large proportion of business written.

Q Having read this section, can you think of the main reasons why new forms of insurance developed?

A The main reasons are in response to a need for cover as new forms of transport developed, new risks arose through the industrial revolution and new forms of cover were designed to meet a perceived need.

A1E Key dates

A useful list of key dates in the history of Lloyd's, from 1688 to the present day has been produced for easy reference:

1688 First known reference to Lloyd's Coffee House in Tower Street.

1720 Royal Charter created monopoly; however, underwriting by private individuals not prohibited (repealed 1824).

1769 Gambling element.
New Lloyd's formed by professional underwriters in Pope's Head Alley.

1771 First Committee of Lloyd's elected nine subscribers.

1774 Rental of 'Rooms' in Royal Exchange. Entry restricted to subscribers and connections.

1796 Resolved by Committee to present annual reports and accounts.

1804 Appointment of first Secretary of Lloyd's.

1811 Trust deed signed by subscribers.
Admission more strictly regulated and Committee increased to twelve.

1857 First deposit made with Committee by underwriting member.

1871 Lloyd's incorporated by Act of Parliament.

1903 First non-marine deposit accepted.

1907 Excess of loss reinsurance introduced by Heath.
'Red Cross' motor policy at Lloyd's.

1908 Annual audit introduced voluntarily and premium trust fund introduced.

1909-46 Assurance Companies Acts made audit and premium trust fund compulsory.

1911 First aviation risk written.

1937 Additional Securities Ltd formed to meet US State legislation requirements.

1939 American trust fund for US dollar premiums.

1980   Fisher Working Party Report published. New Lloyd's Bill drafted, based on Fisher proposals.

1982   Royal Assent received for Lloyd's Act 1982 on 23 July. Election of first Council of Lloyd's in November, appointment of three nominated members in December.

1986   Neill Committee of Inquiry established to consider whether the regulatory arrangements at Lloyd's provided protection for names comparable to that proposed for investors under the Financial Services Act 1986.

1987   Report of the Neill Committee of Inquiry published.
Launch of London Insurance Market Network (LIMNET).

1988   Lloyd's tercentenary (300th anniversary).

1992   'Lloyd's: A Route Forward' Task Force Report published.

B

THE LLOYD'S MARKET

Lloyd's is both a Society and an insurance market place:

Lloyd's, a Society

The Lloyd's Act 1871 incorporated the Society into a 'Society and Corporation'. No distinction has been made between the Society and Corporation in that Act or any subsequent Acts; in legal terms, they are one and the same entity, comprising the members of Lloyd's for the time being and all rights and all property that are collectively theirs.

Lloyd's, an insurance market

Lloyd's is an insurance market where, with few exceptions (notably long-term life and certain financial guarantee business), any insurable risk can be placed with Lloyd's underwriters through Lloyd's brokers. Certain business may be placed directly with Lloyd's syndicates by non-Lloyd's intermediaries or through service companies set up by managing agencies.

B1 ORGANISATION OF THE MARKET

Insurances are placed not with the Corporation of Lloyd's, but with members of the Society (also known as ♦**names**♦. These underwriting members alone are entitled to accept insurance business.

In the eighteenth century, underwriters carried on their business singly and each man accepted risks for himself alone. In more recent years, members joined together with groups, called syndicates, so that the resources of a large number of underwriters were combined into a single unit. This arrangement enabled them to deal in much larger sums than before and also widened their scope enormously. Each syndicate member is individually liable to the full extent of his private means for his own share of risks accepted; he is not liable in respect of other members' shares.

♦**Managing agents**♦ manage the underwriting affairs of these syndicates and their underwriting representative sits at his box in the Room and accepts business on behalf of the members of the syndicate. Some agents underwrite for more than one syndicate.

♦**Members' agents**♦ have the responsibility for bringing in suitable new members to join these syndicates and thus increase their capacity to write business. They also act in all respects on behalf of their names, except in the management of the syndicate, which is the responsibility of the managing agency.

The four principle classes of business are:

- ▶ marine;
- ▶ non-marine;
- ▶ motor;
- ▶ aviation.

B1A Marine

Marine is the oldest class at Lloyd's and is still regarded as the leading world marine market, covering anything from oil production platforms to yachts, dating back 300 years to the coffee house days.

B1B Non-marine

Non-marine business owes its great expansion to Cuthbert Heath who in the 1890s introduced earthquake, burglary, loss of profits and jewellers' block policies, etc. Today, this market accounts for nearly half the premium income of Lloyd's under-writers.

B1C Motor

Motor insurance covers all facets of the insurance of road vehicles in the UK and certain territories over-seas. It is estimated that more than one in seven British private motorists are insured at Lloyd's.

B1D Aviation

Aviation insurance provides insurance for all types of aircraft from helicopters, jumbo jets and Concorde, to passenger liabilities and communication satellites.

B2 MEMBERS

Each underwriting member is fully and personally liable for his share for all the business written on behalf of his syndicate by the underwriter whom it employs. In view of this unlimited liability, it is ess-ential that strict regulations apply to any person wishing to become an underwriting member. The current rules are governed by bye-laws passed by the Council of Lloyd's. A special high level stop loss scheme fund has been set up from 1 January 1993 to protect members against exceptional losses.

Persons wishing to become members must have their application sponsored by two existing mem-bers, one of whom must be a director/partner or employee of the proposed members' agent. They must also show that they are persons of sufficient wealth and over 21 years of age. The application can only be made through a registered members' agent. Candidates, who may be men or women of any nationality, go before a ◆**Rota Committee**◆ for

interview and, if approved, their applications are further considered by the appropriate body prior to final election.

Prior to election a member pays an entrance fee and lodges certain ◆**funds at Lloyd's**◆ which are held in trust by the members' agent's trustees and/or the Corporation. The administration of these funds is the responsibility of the members' agent together with the Corporation. The amount of a prospective member's funds at Lloyd's is related to his ◆**overall premium limit**◆ in accordance with ratios laid down by the Council of Lloyd's. These funds at Lloyd's are part of the security underlying the Lloyd's insurance policy.

A statement of means proving acceptable wealth must be provided prior to election, and a member must maintain at all times his means at the level required by the Council.

Those members not involved in day-to-day business at Lloyd's are defined as ◆**external members**◆ while those working at Lloyd's are defined as ◆**working members**◆. Members must pay an annual subscription based on their allocated overall premium income limits, and this is collected through the managing agents acting for them. These fees are used by the Council of Lloyd's to defray the Corporation of Lloyd's expenses.

All underwriting premiums received by a member of Lloyd's must be paid into a ◆**premiums trust fund**◆, in the United States for dollar premiums, Canada for Canadian dollar premiums, or in the United Kingdom for other premiums.

Only claims, reinsurance premiums, expenses and ascertained profits may be paid from these funds which are administered by trustees, at least one of whom is the member's underwriting agent.

In addition to a member's deposit and his premium trust fund, a portion of the profits earned is often retained in trust for a member as an additional reserve against underwriting losses. This reserve may take the form of a ◆**personal reserve**◆ agreed with the underwriting agent and/or a ◆**special reserve fund**◆ treated according to conditions agreed by the UK Board of Inland Revenue.

B3 LLOYD'S BROKERS

Business is brought to Lloyd's by firms of Lloyd's brokers who are not restricted to dealing with Lloyd's underwriters, but may place business with insurance companies as well.

The client approaches the broker and gives him details of his insurance requirements. The broker advises the client on the type of cover he wants and puts brief details of the risk on a ◆**slip**◆. Having made out the slip, the broker goes into the market and approaches one or more ◆**leading under-writers**◆ who specialise in the type of risk he is trying to place. The underwriter asks the broker questions about the risk and suggests a rate of premium. Bargaining may take place, with the broker trying to get the best terms for his client. When a premium rate is agreed, the underwriter takes a ◆**line**◆ by writing on the slip the share of the risk he is prepared to accept for his syndicate, together with the premium and his initials. Once the broker has got the risk started by a recognised lead he can then approach other underwriters to take a share and to sign at the same rate until he completes the cover.

The broker may **over-complete** the risk in order to provide for any future increase in sums insured or limits of liability which may be required and to give as many underwriters as possible the chance to go on the risk; each syndicate's proportion is afterwards scaled down so that the total coverage is finally 100%.

The broker operates at all times in the interest of his client and must understand his requirements and advise on the best way to meet them. It is the duty of the broker to obtain the best possible terms for his clients whether at Lloyd's or in the insurance company market in London or elsewhere, or both. Should there be a claim, the broker arranges the settlement, collects the money from the underwriters and pays it out in the appropriate quarter. The premium income of Lloyd's underwriters depends on the energy and enterprise of the brokers working in harmony with the judgment and experience of the underwriters.

Lloyd's underwriters draw their business from every continent and most countries of the world; there are few places in which it is not possible to find firms or individuals with contacts among Lloyd's brokers through whom business can be placed at Lloyd's.

B4 THE CORPORATION OF LLOYD'S

As we have seen, the Society of Lloyd's was incorporated by Act of Parliament in the year 1871. The Act provided, *inter alia*, for the objects of the Society, the establishment of a Committee and the making of bye-laws. The Corporation of Lloyd's does not underwrite insurance business. Its function is to provide the premises, services and assistance necessary for the conduct of underwriting, and to assist in the regulation of the market place.

SUMMARY

In this chapter we have traced the development of Lloyd's and set the scene for a more detailed study of the market. In the following chapter we will examine self-regulation at Lloyd's, the position of Lloyd's brokers, members, the syndicate system and the approval of underwriting agents.

6

GLOSSARY OF TERMS

External member
A member of the Society who is not a working member of the Society.

Funds at Lloyd's
This includes the Lloyd's deposit, personal reserves and special reserves.

Leading underwriter
An underwriter whose judgment is so respected by other underwriters that they will follow his lead in accepting a risk. His syndicate will appear first on the slip.

Line
The sum or percentage written on a broker's slip on behalf of the syndicate of names for whom he acts, which establishes the proportion of the risk accepted by an underwriter.

Managing agent
A managing agent is a person who is permitted by the Council in the conduct of his business as an underwriting agent to perform for an underwriting member one or more of the following functions:

- ▶ underwriting contracts of insurance at Lloyd's;
- ▶ reinsuring such contracts in whole or in part;
- ▶ paying claims on such contracts.

Members' agent
An underwriting agent who acts in all respects for the name, except in the management of the syndicate.

Name
An underwriting member whose name appears on the list of those participating in any syndicate at Lloyd's.

Overall premium limit
The maximum amount of business which a member may underwrite based on the levels of his funds at Lloyd's. The limit is allocated to syndicates in proportions agreed between the member and the members' agent.

Personal reserve
A fund retained by the underwriting agent on behalf of a member as security for his underwriting liabilities.

Premiums trust fund (PTF)
A trust fund required under the United Kingdom Insurance Companies Act, into which all premiums and other underwriting monies must be paid.

Rota Committee
A committee established to interview applicants for underwriting membership or for admission as a Lloyd's broker or underwriting agent.

Slip
A document submitted by a broker to underwriters, containing particulars of a risk proposed for insurance.

Special reserve fund
An arrangement under the Income Tax Acts, whereby a proportion of underwriting profit and certain investment income can be placed to reserve with relief from or deferral of higher rate tax. The fund is available for relief for future losses only.

Working member
▶ A member of the Society who occupies himself primarily with the conduct of business at Lloyd's by a Lloyd's broker or underwriting agent.

▶ A member of the Society who has gone into retirement but who immediately before his retirement so occupies himself.

6

MULTIPLE CHOICE QUESTIONS

1.   Which of the following statements is correct?

    (a)   Lloyd's began in 1804.
    (b)   Lloyd's began in the mid-sixteenth century.
    (c)   Lloyd's began in the Coffee House in Tower Street in 1811.
    (d)   Lloyd's began towards the end of the seventeenth century.

2.   Women have been allowed to be members of Lloyd's since:

    (a)   Queen Victoria's accession to the throne in 1832;
    (b)   women were given the vote;
    (c)   the late 1960s;
    (d)   February 1974.

Which of these alternatives is correct?

3.   The Lloyd's Act of 1982 was drafted largely from the recommendations of the:

    (a)   Bird Working Party;
    (b)   Fisher Working Party;
    (c)   Corporation of Lloyd's;
    (d)   Council of Lloyd's.

Which of the above is correct?

4.   Lloyd's annual audit was introduced voluntarily. Which Act of Parliament to regulate insurers did it immediately precede?

    (a)   The Assurance Companies Act 1909.
    (b)   The Assurance Companies Act 1946.
    (c)   The Insurance Companies Act 1958.
    (d)   The Lloyd's Act 1982.

5.   In 1769 the new Lloyd's was formed by professional underwriters in Pope's Head Alley. This was necessary because:

    (a)   the Committee decided that better premises were required;
    (b)   gambling insurances were being written in the existing Lloyd's;
    (c)   the first Lloyd's Act of Parliament was passed in that year;
    (d)   underwriters wished to expand their business to write non-marine risks.

6

MULTIPLE CHOICE QUESTIONS

6. In the late nineteenth century, Cuthbert Heath:

    (a) proposed the formation of the first syndicate; ☐

    (b) drafted the Act of Parliament (1871) which incorporated the Society of Lloyd's; ☐

    (c) insured the first motor vehicle covered by a Lloyd's underwriter; ☐

    (d) was largely responsible for the expansion of the non-marine market. ☑

7. Which of the statements below is inaccurate?

    (a) Applicants for membership of Lloyd's must be sponsored by two existing underwriting members. ☐

    (b) Applicants for membership of Lloyd's must be over 21 and of sufficient wealth. ☐

    (c) Final election is by ballot. ☐

    (d) Applicants must be resident in the UK. ☑

8. Which of the following statements about the Corporation of Lloyd's is false?

    (a) The Corporation is financed by an annual grant from HM Treasury. ☑

    (b) The Corporation does not underwrite insurance business. ☐

    (c) The Corporation provides the premises, assistance and services for the conduct of underwriting. ☐

    (d) The Corporation regulates the operation of the market place. ☐

9. Which of the following committees of Lloyd's interviews all prospective applicants, prior to their election to become members of Lloyd's?

    (a) Names' Interests Committee. ☐

    (b) Investigations Committee. ☐

    (c) Solvency and Security Committee. ☐

    (d) Rota Committee. ☑

ANSWERS TO MULTIPLE CHOICE QUESTIONS APPEAR OVERLEAF

ANSWERS TO MULTIPLE CHOICE QUESTIONS

1. Answer (d), Lloyd's began towards the end of the seventeenth century.

2. Answer (c), the late 1960s.

3. Answer (b), Fisher Working Party.

4. Answer (a), Assurance Companies Act 1909.

5. Answer (b), gambling insurances were being written in the existing Lloyd's.

6. Answer (d), Cuthbert Heath was largely responsible for the expansion of the non-marine market.

7. Answer (d).

8. Answer (a), because the Corporation is not financed by an annual grant from HM Treasury.

9. Answer (d), Rota Committee.

7

REGULATION OF THE LLOYD'S MARKET

LEARNING OBJECTIVES

After studying this chapter, you should be able to:

▷ identify the purpose and nature of self-regulation at Lloyd's;

▷ discuss the powers of the Council, Market and Regulatory Boards;

▷ distinguish between primary and secondary rules;

▷ write brief notes on the approval and respective duties of members' and managing agencies;

▷ identify the responsibilities of and principal requirements for a Lloyd's broking firm.

INTRODUCTION

In this chapter we will consider the nature of self-regulation, the Lloyd's Act 1982 and the ruling bodies within Lloyd's. We will also consider the security of Lloyd's policies and the requirements to become a Lloyd's broking firm and an underwriting agency.

Lloyd's is a self-regulatory organisation, but must comply with various sections of the Insurance Companies Act 1982 and, of course, the Society is controlled by the Lloyd's Act 1982.

A

SELF-REGULATION AT LLOYD'S

We will consider the nature of self-regulation, the Lloyd's Act 1982 and the ruling bodies within Lloyd's. We will conclude by discussing primary and secondary rules.

A1 THE NATURE OF SELF-REGULATION

The effectiveness of any form of regulation depends upon the general willingness of society to obey the law and respect the sanctions which the regulatory body is prepared to enforce. There are broadly two ways to do this:

► statutory regulation; and
► self-regulation.

? How does self-regulation differ from statutory regulation?

Self-regulation differs in essence from statutory regulation in that it is a system of rule-making devised and operated by those to whom the rules are applied. Such regulation is thus of limited scope and designed to apply to and regulate members of a defined group. It also lays down standards of conduct which a statute could not easily cover.

A1A Objectives of self-regulation at Lloyd's

The objectives identified by the **Fisher Working Party**, which was appointed by the Committee of Lloyd's in 1978 to enquire into the self-regulation of

Lloyd's and chaired by Sir Henry Fisher, were reported in 1980. The Working Party was concerned with:

> **...the maintenance of the security of the Lloyd's policy, the maintenance of the highest standards of conduct and integrity by all users of the market, the preservation of Lloyd's as a market where conditions of free competition can obtain, and the maintenance of standards of fair treatment for those members of the Lloyd's community who can reasonably look to the Committee for protection.**

Figure 7.1: Objectives of self-regulation

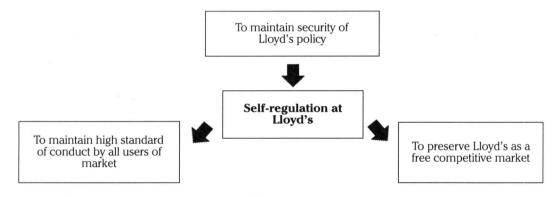

A number of key factors must be taken into account in the regulation of Lloyd's:

▶ There is a **diversity of interests.** Regulation at Lloyd's is not simply a matter of providing protection for names. It is a complex operation involving the balancing of diverse interests amongst which are, pre-eminently, the protection of policyholders and the provision and the maintenance of an efficient, flexible and innovative market as well as the protection of members.

▶ **Standards** have to be applied. Lloyd's has a long tradition of free enterprise. The market has always adhered to the principle that the 'authorities' should refrain from interference with commercial decisions, unless absolutely necessary, so as to permit development and change in response to commercial pressures. This can only be justified where high standards of conduct are followed.

▶ There is the question of **flexibility** and the element of **judgment**. Flexibility is important not only because of the innovative nature of the market, but also because of the need to keep Lloyd's rules and standards up-to-date so that they reflect changes in standards and expectations generally. All the other points mentioned above depend in some measure upon the exercise of wise judgement.

▶ The pervasive existence of **agency relationships** within Lloyd's will strongly influence the form and substance of regulation. For example, members can only write business through agencies and usually insurance business may only be placed via Lloyd's brokers. Lloyd's regulations must both take account of this and reinforce the standards required of an agent.

A2 LLOYD'S ACT 1982

The Lloyd's Act 1982 repealed many of the provisions of the earlier Acts and it has given effect to the central recommendations of the Fisher Working Party Report. It provided for the establishment of the Council of Lloyd's, charged with overall responsibility for and control of the affairs of the Society, including, specifically, all rule-making and disciplinary powers, hitherto vested in the membership as a whole.

The 1982 Act was, essentially, an enabling measure providing a framework for the regulation of the Society, and we will consider the Council, the Regulatory Board and the Market Board and their powers and functions in the following sections.

A3 COUNCIL OF LLOYD'S

Until the end of 1992, the Council of Lloyd's comprised 28 members (27 were provided for under the 1982 Act, but this number was increased by bye-law).

The **Morse Report**, entitled A New Structure of Governance for Lloyd's', recommended reducing the size of the Council from 28 to 14 members and the separation of its regulatory and business functions. The Council of Lloyd's made some modifications to the Morse Working Party's recommendations which were themselves based on the recommendations of the Lloyd's Task Force Report, published in 1992. These were that the Chief Executive Officer and the Head of Regulation should be nominated members of the Council so that Council would, at 1 January 1995, comprise 16 members.

The Council structure is as follows:

Working members
These are members of the Council, elected from and by the working members of the Society. A working member is a member of the Society who occupies himself principally with the conduct of the business of insurance at Lloyd's carried out by a Lloyd's broker or underwriting agent or who so occupied himself immediately before retirement.

External members
External members of the Council are elected from and by the external members of the Society. An external member is defined as being a member of the Society who is not a working member of the Society.

Nominated members
These are not members of the Society but are persons appointed by the Council. Any such appointment requires confirmation by the Governor of the Bank of England. One nominated member is the current Chairman (or a Deputy Chairman) of the Securities and Investments Board.

The Act requires the annual appointment by the Council of a Chairman and two or more Deputy Chairmen of the Council, from amongst the working members of the Council. The Chairman of Lloyd's will be a paid position from 1993 for the first time.

Figure 7.2: The structure of the Council of Lloyd's

Chairman (working member)		
Deputy chairman (working member)	Deputy chairman (nominated member)	Deputy chairman (working member)

plus

Working members	External members	Nominated members

A3A Transitional arrangements

The transitional arrangements to arrive at the size of Council envisaged by the modified Morse proposals are as follows:

	Working	External	Nominated	Total
1.1.93	8	5	8	21
1.1.94	6	4	7	17
1.1.95	6	4	6	16

A3B Powers of the Council

The Lloyd's Act 1982 states that the Council shall have the management and superintendence of the affairs of the Society and the power to regulate and direct the business of insurance at Lloyd's, and provides that it may make such bye-laws as may seem requisite or expedient. These powers are also subject, under some circumstances, to review by a general meeting of the Society.

The Morse Working Party proposals do not affect the status of Council as the senior and legislative body of the Society. However, under the Working Party's proposals, Council will discharge many of its other duties through a Market Board and a Regulatory board (see sections A4A and A4B below) and will normally accept the recommendations of these boards. Council itself will make bye-laws, maintain a disciplinary system and resolve any matters upon which the two boards are unable to reach agreement. It will determine all entrance fees, subscriptions and levies and will approve and monitor budgets of the Corporation and its subsidiaries. It remains ultimately responsible for the affairs of the Society.

A4 TRIPARTITE STRUCTURE

The Morse Working Party recommended a new tripartite structure for Lloyd's, namely the Council of Lloyd's, and the establishment of a Regulatory Board and a Market Board.

It should be noted, however, that the Committee of Lloyd's remains in existence as provided under the Lloyd's Act 1982. The Committee comprises the working members of Council and, whilst most of its former functions will now be discharged by the Market Board, it retains its responsibility for making regulations and giving directions on technical insurance matters. The working members of Council will be members both of the Market Board and of the Committee of Lloyd's. It is envisaged that they will meet as the Committee of Lloyd's relatively infrequently.

A4A Market Board

The Market Board was described in the Morse Report as the driving force in the development of Lloyd's business with its own responsibility for compliance. Its primary purpose is to advance the interests of Lloyd's members in the conduct of insurance business and it will lead and organise the Society's collective efforts in this regard. It is chaired by the Chairman of Lloyd's. The membership of the Market Board is made up of the following: *18 members -*

- ▶ six voting members of the Council;
- ▶ up to four representatives of the underwriting associations;
- ▶ one representative of the underwriting agents association;
- ▶ one representative of the Lloyd's brokers association;
- ▶ two or three non-executive members (yet to be determined);
- ▶ the Chief Executive Officer, supported by two senior Corporation executives.

A4B Regulatory Board

The Morse Report described the Regulatory Board as an informed monitor and facilitator for putting in place an appropriate regulatory structure for the market's business.

The primary purpose of the Board is to provide and administer a set of rules which protect the interests of Lloyd's members whilst upholding their contractual obligation to policyholders and others, and legal requirements in countries where they do business.

The Board is chaired by a nominated member of Council, with the title of Deputy Chairman. ~~Up to~~ 16 members ~~may~~ serve on the Regulatory Board, the breakdown being as follows:

- ▶ four working members appointed by Council;
- ▶ four external members of Council;

6

▶ five nominated members (including the Head of Regulation);

▶ the solicitor to the Corporation;

▶ two additional members, if appointed by Council.

A5 THE CORPORATION OF LLOYD'S

Although it was established by the Lloyd's Act 1871 under the 'Society and Corporation', the Corporation may trace its beginnings to 1771, when the merchant underwriters first resolved to run the premises themselves through an elected committee. However, it was not until 1804 that the first administrative staff member was appointed.

As we have seen, the Corporation of Lloyd's does not underwrite insurance business. Its function is to provide the premises, services and assistance necessary for the conduct of underwriting and to assist in the regulation of the market place.

Figure 7.3: The functions of the Corporation

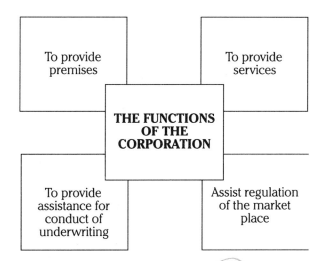

The Corporation of Lloyd's is divided into seven groups, each managed by a 'group head'. The responsibilities of each group are as follows:

▶ **Finance**. This group is responsible for the Corporation's financial and taxation affairs and represents the interests of the Society in taxation issues affecting names or syndicates. It also provides certain financial services to the market.

▶ **Solicitor to the Corporation**. This group provides legal advice to the Council and Corporation. It is also responsible for the conduct of investigations and for the conduct of proceedings before Lloyd's Disciplinary Committees and Appeal Tribunal.

▶ **Market Services**. This group provides general services to the market. The largest department in the group is Lloyd's Policy Signing Office. Other departments are International, Lloyd's Claims Office, Agency and Aviation.

▶ **Systems and Communications**. This group provides computer and telecommunications services to the market and is responsible for developing systems to aid both the market and the Corporation in its work.

▶ **Administration**. Within this group are the departments responsible for providing premises, catering and training for the market and for the Corporation's administration and personnel function.

▶ **Public Affairs**. The Public Affairs Department is concerned with media relations, Lloyd's publications, parliamentary liaison and the visitors' exhibition, amongst other responsibilities.

▶ **Regulatory Services**. The Corporation's function in the self-regulation of Lloyd's is largely performed by departments within this group. Responsibilities include membership matters, registration and continued supervision of underwriting agents and Lloyd's brokers, approval of arrangements for the introduction of business, preparation of statutory reports, registration of auditors, protection of Lloyd's trading position and handling of customer complaints.

A6 HOW SELF-REGULATION OPERATES AT LLOYD'S

Lloyd's traditionally has operated through a committee structure both for the development of rules and their implementation. Proposals emanating from committees will be considered by the Market or Regulatory Boards (as appropriate) who may refer them to Council if, for example, legislative action is required. The Committee of Lloyd's may make regulations on technical insurance matters.

A6A The structure of 'rules' at Lloyd's

We will now consider the structure of 'rules' at Lloyd's which range from bye-laws to codes of best practice.

Various types of 'rules' have been developed under the specific and general powers contained in the Lloyd's Act. These are:

▶ **primary rules**, that is, bye-laws and regulations;

▶ **secondary rules**, which encompass explanatory notes and codes of practice.

A6A1 Primary rules

Bye-laws may:

▶ cover matters of principle fundamental to Lloyd's;
▶ clarify disciplinary matters;
▶ be procedural; or
▶ establish rules of the Society.

Regulations apply the bye-laws to specific market circumstances.

Bye-laws and regulations may be made independently of each other or may be inter-related. For example, a bye-law may be passed which is widely drawn and expressed in general terms. Thereafter, a regulation is drawn up to assist in the detailed application and interpretation of the bye-law in specific market circumstances.

A6A2 Secondary rules

The policy of the Council is to avoid, as far as possible, detailed primary rules and to keep the content of bye-laws and regulations to a minimum. Many of Lloyd's bye-laws are enabling in nature and are confirmed to the general principles involved. Secondary rules are designed to back up, or fill in the detail of, such primary rules and to be capable of speedy amendment.

This structure permits the general principle expressed in the primary rules to survive without alteration for some time and for secondary rules to be expanded or amended as and when policy changes occur or problems arise.

Explanatory notes are not 'rules' as such, but form part of the regulatory structure and are issued to explain the intention of a bye-law or regulation.

Similarly, codes of practice are not strictly 'rules' in that they do not categorically prohibit or require. The purpose of a code of practice is to try to raise the standards of those covered by the code to those of the best and to spell out those standards of behaviour which it would be in the interests of the Lloyd's community to achieve.

No disciplinary action would flow from breach of the provisions of a code, although regard would be had to its contents in any disciplinary proceedings.

B

REGULATION OF LLOYD'S BROKERS

We will now consider briefly the regulation of Lloyd's brokers. Although a detailed study of the Lloyd's Brokers Bye-law is beyond the scope of this course, it is important that you have an outline knowledge.

B1 REGULATION OF LLOYD'S BROKERS

Contracts of insurance at Lloyd's cannot be effected directly between the proposers and Lloyd's underwriters with the exception of:

▶ certain personal lines business or commercial motor business which may be accepted from non-Lloyd's intermediaries or where personal lines or commercial motor business is accepted by a service company set up by a managing agency to deal direct with the public with no involvement by a Lloyd's broker;

▶ risks placed through umbrella brokers who have umbrella arrangements with Lloyd's brokers.

They can only be transacted through insurance brokers styled 'Lloyd's brokers' who are registered by the Council under the Lloyd's Brokers Bye-law. All Lloyd's brokers are required to enrol with the Insurance Brokers Registration Council, established under the ◆ **Insurance Brokers (Registration) Act 1977** ◆.

Virtually all the Council's powers to regulate Lloyd's brokers are delegated to the Broker Registration Committee. This is a committee of the Council and includes representatives of both brokers and underwriters. Brokers also operate under the code of practice for Lloyd's brokers and are committed to additional responsibilities on behalf of Lloyd's underwriters beyond normal insurance broking practice and within the general law of agency.

B2 LLOYD'S BROKERS BYE-LAW

The Lloyd's Brokers Bye-law provides for the grant of permission to broke insurance business at Lloyd's by virtue of the registration of a corporate body or partnership as a Lloyd's broker and for the review, renewal and withdrawal of such registration. Subject to certain exceptions, the bye-law prohibits the broking of insurance business at Lloyd's by any firm which is not registered under the bye-law.

The Lloyd's Brokers Bye-law empowers the Council to impose conditions and make requirements regarding Lloyd's brokers' financial resources and their maintenance of professional indemnity insurance, requires Lloyd's brokers to maintain and use insurance broking accounts and makes provision regarding accounting records, accounts and other reports, audit and an annual return.

The bye-law empowers the Council to require the execution of deeds or other instruments by Lloyd's brokers for the purpose of protecting the interests of their insurance creditors and to establish a scheme to provide for run-off costs.

B3 REQUIREMENTS FOR BECOMING A 'LLOYD'S BROKING FIRM'

An applicant firm will not be registered as a Lloyd's broker unless the Council is satisfied that:

▶ the applicant firm complies with the requirements of the Lloyd's Brokers Bye-law, and every other bye-law and regulation for the time being in force and applicable to it;

▶ the applicant firm is registered by the ◆ **Insurance Brokers Registration Council (IBRC)** ◆; and

▶ the applicant firm is fit and proper to be a Lloyd's broker.

Also there must not be any arrangement which might enable the applicant to influence the policy or business of a managing agency, or *vice versa*, other than a normal commercial arrangement. This is the result of the divestment provisions under the Lloyd's Act 1982 where Lloyd's brokers were banned from having an interest in managing agencies or *vice versa*.

B3A Competence

In deciding whether an applicant firm is fit and proper to be a Lloyd's broker, the Council will consider, amongst other factors, the following:

▶ the character and suitability of the directors and partners;

▶ the sufficiency in number of directors and partners experienced in Lloyd's business whose principal occupation it is;

▶ the reputation, character and suitability of any person who controls the applicant firm;

▶ the adequacy of the capital of the applicant firm;

▶ whether the business is or is likely to become unduly dependent on a particular insurer or insurers or a particular source of business;

▶ the ability of the applicant firms to supervise and service its activities; and

▶ the location, adequacy and suitability of staff.

B3B Review

All firms registered will be reviewed from time to time. A Lloyd's broker may be removed from the register if it:

▶ fails to comply with the requirements of the Lloyd's Brokers Bye-law;

▶ is not a fit and proper body to be a Lloyd's broker;

▶ ceases to broke business at Lloyd's; or

▶ fails to comply with a condition specifically imposed on it by the Council or at its own request.

Directors must be underwriting members or annual subscribers and no Lloyd's broker can carry on any business other than that of insurance broking and such other business as the Council considers to be directly ancillary to insurance broking.

Every Lloyd's broker should appoint a person to be responsible for compliance by the Lloyd's broker with Lloyd's Acts 1871 to 1982, the bye-laws and regulations made under those Acts and for ensuring that the Lloyd's broker pays due regard to any codes of practice, market circulars or other advice issued by or under the authority of the Council or Committee. The person appointed must be a director or partner, unless the Council agrees otherwise.

B3C Financial aspects

Transactions with related parties, such as an insurance company connected with the Lloyd's broker, must be disclosed to the proposer. The Council has powers to prescribe conditions and requirements regarding the possession and maintenance by Lloyd's brokers of financial resources considered appropriate.

Every Lloyd's broker must establish and maintain one or more separate bank accounts, termed ◆**insurance broking accounts (IBAs)**◆. Each insurance broking account must be maintained with an approved bank and be used for monies received for insurance transactions and payments of such monies to insureds and insurers.

B3D Accounting requirements

Proper accounting records shall be kept and preserved by all broking firms whether the Companies Act 1985 applies or not. All such accounts will be examined by an auditor and an annual return filed with the Society of Lloyd's. Professional indemnity insurance is compulsory for all Lloyd's brokers. Every Lloyd's broker shall make and retain records of all contracts of insurance arranged by it. Council shall be notified of changes in directors, partners and compliance officers and its prior consent obtained for new appointments.

B3E The agency broker

In certain cases an ◆**agency broker**◆, carrying on insurance business exclusively as an agent for a Lloyd's insurance broker, may be granted permission to broke business at Lloyd's, although it may not fulfill all the criteria for a registered Lloyd's broker.

B4 UMBRELLA ARRANGEMENTS

An ◆**umbrella arrangement**◆ is an arrangement between a Lloyd's broker and a non-Lloyd's broker whereby the non-Lloyd's broker is permitted to use the name, LPSO number or pseudonym of the Lloyd's broker for placing insurance business with or on behalf of (in the case of syndicate reinsurance) underwriting members.

A bye-law regularises the position and these arrangements are only permitted in two situations:

▶ where the non-Lloyd's broker is a subsidiary of a Lloyd's broker; and

▶ in respect of a non-Lloyd's broker which has the intention of becoming a Lloyd's broker within three years of being registered under such arrangements.

The non-Lloyd's broker must be registered with the Insurance Brokers Registration Council.

There must be an undertaking given by the Lloyd's broker to the Council adequately to supervise the non-Lloyd's broker; a written agreement must be in force between the Lloyd's and non-Lloyd's brokers; and the non-Lloyd's broker and its directors must give an undertaking in the form laid down by the Council.

B5 THE LLOYD'S BROKER: AGENT OF THE INSURED

With the exception of the acceptance of risks and issuance of documents under binding authorities and some services in claims negotiations and issuing certificates in motor insurance, the broker is always the agent of the insured in Lloyd's transactions. All the common law duties of disclosure and utmost good faith apply to brokers and their clients as well as insurers in contracts of non-marine, aviation and motor insurance at Lloyd's, while for certain marine contracts these duties are made statutory by the Marine Insurance Act 1906.

C

MEMBERSHIP

Each underwriting member is fully and personally liable for his share of all the business written on behalf of his syndicate by the underwriter whom it employs. In view of this unlimited liability, it is essential that strict regulations apply to any person wishing to become an underwriting member.

A special high level stop loss scheme fund has been set up with effect from 1 January 1993 to protect members against exceptional losses.

C1 REQUIREMENTS OF MEMBERSHIP

There are various categories of membership at Lloyd's. Each member must show funds at Lloyd's as a percentage of his overall premium limit. Of these funds, a proportion must be lodged as a minimum deposit at Lloyd's. The minimum means for external members elected from 1 Janauary 1993 is £250,000.

Members must notify the Co<del>mmittee</del> of Lloyd's should their net worth fall below the required level. If a member is unable to satisfy the Committee at any time regarding his means, the Committee may require the member to cease underwriting or to reduce his overall premium limit for such period as it thinks fit. Those who are actively employed full-time in the Lloyd's market (subject to certain qualifying criteria) can be admitted as members with higher percentage funds at Lloyd's without having to show means; however, the amount of their permitted overall premium limit is restricted. The means test must be signed by the applicant as well as by an approved bank with a branch in the United Kingdom, by a practising firm of United Kingdom solicitors, chartered or certified accountants or their associated firms or the applicant's members' agent. The means test must be in 'readily realisable' assets, as defined by the Council of Lloyd's.

Figure 7.4: Name's declared assets

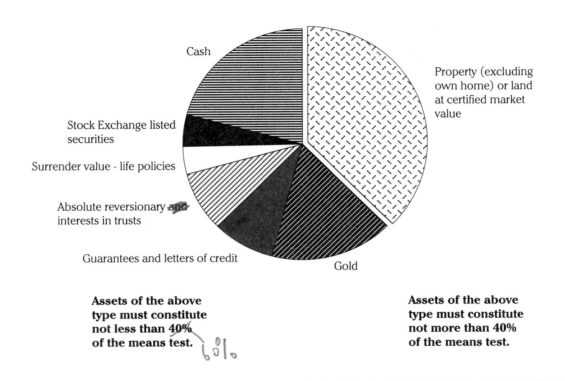

Cash

Property (excluding own home) or land at certified market value

Stock Exchange listed securities

Surrender value - life policies

Absolute reversionary and interests in trusts

Guarantees and letters of credit

Gold

Assets of the above type must constitute not less than 40% of the means test. 60%

Assets of the above type must constitute not more than 40% of the means test.

D

SECURITY UNDERLYING POLICIES AT LLOYD'S

The first priority of Lloyd's has always been the security of the policy, since the protection of the policyholder is seen as paramount. Each individual link in the chain of security behind each Lloyd's policy is strictly policed and adds to the overall protection enjoyed by the policyholder. These links are set out below.

D1 THE CHAIN OF SECURITY

Individual unlimited liability

Members of Lloyd's accept insurance business solely for their own account and there is no joint liability between the individual members. Members' liability to pay claims which arise from their share of the risks is unlimited up to the total amount of their personal wealth. **It is this basic principle of individual unlimited liability which lies at the heart of Lloyd's**.

A high level **stop loss scheme** for members has been introduced from 1 January 1993. If total net losses of a member over a four year period exceed 80% of the overall premium limit, the losses above that level will be met by a fund specially set up under the scheme. Members make annual contributions to the fund based on the syndicate's allocated capacity for the year of account.

normally

Members' personal wealth

The member's total personal wealth forms the bedrock capital that supports their underwriting. Prior to joining Lloyd's, each prospective member must provide independent verification of a minimum level of readily realisable assets (qualifying means). This is a minimum level of wealth and it may reasonably be inferred that the actual wealth of members exceeds this figure, probably by a substantial amount.

Members' funds at Lloyd's

Before a member can commence underwriting, a specified amount of assets must be placed in trust at Lloyd's to support the member's agreed overall premium limit (OPL) for that year in accordance with ratios laid down by the Council of Lloyd's. These funds are known as **'funds at Lloyd's'**. The administration of these funds is the responsibility of the agent and/or the Corporation as laid down by the various trust deeds and regulatory requirements. These funds must be in a form approved by the Council of Lloyd's and maintained in value.

The funds may consist of cash, approved investments or a guarantee/letter of credit from a bank, approved building society or insurance company as security for underwriting commitments.

In addition, a member may hold assets in excess of these regulatory requirements in his personal reserve fund if considered necessary by his members' agent.

At the beginning of each calendar year any member with the agreement of their underwriting agent may increase the amount of their funds and therefore their overall premium limit. A member may be required by the Council to provide an additional security where his premium income in the previous year exceeds his total permitted overall premium limit.

In the event that there are insufficient monies in their premiums trust funds, the funds which the members have established in respect of their underwriting may be used in certain circumstances towards meeting their liabilities.

Premiums trust funds

All premiums received from policyholders together with consequent investment income must be held in a trust fund in accordance with the provisions of a premiums trust deed approved by the Secretary of State. Lloyd's operates separate trusts in three currencies:

- ▶ Sterling Premium Trust Fund in UK;
- ▶ Lloyd's American Trust Fund (LATF) held in USA;
- ▶ Lloyd's Canadian Trust Fund (LCTF) held in Canada.

Profits can only be distributed to members from these funds after a period has been determined, having regard to all known and estimated future liabilities

calculated on a basis approved by the Secretary of State. Under the Lloyd's three year accounting method a result for each syndicate is not calculated earlier than three years after the start of the account, with each year's business being treated as a separate account. If a loss is determined then it has to be funded by members from their personal resources at this time.

Lloyd's Central Fund

Individual members are liable for their own underwriting commitments but should the assets held in trust on their behalf at Lloyd's, or their own personal resources, prove insufficient to meet their liabilities, there are resources held centrally which are available to meet their underwriting obligations. These resources consist of the ♦ **Central Fund** ♦ to which all members pay an annual levy, and the assets of the Corporation of Lloyd's. These assets provide the ultimate safeguard and protection for the Lloyd's policyholder in the event of a member failing to meet his underwriting obligations.

The Central Fund Bye-law provides for its use for any purpose which, in the Council's opinion, is in the interests of the members of Lloyd's as a whole in connection with their underwriting business.

D1A Investment regulations

Lloyd's specifies investment regulations in respect of both 'funds at Lloyd's' and 'premiums trust funds'. Lloyd's takes a very prudent approach towards acceptable assets, and regulations ensure that funds are invested in high quality assets which are readily realisable.

D1B Security controls

In addition to the level of assets which back Lloyd's policies there are strict controls on the underwriting activities of members, which are monitored by Lloyd's.

Controls are exercised by the Lloyd's solvency test and the overall premium limit, which is the maximum amount of business which a member may underwrite based on the level of his funds at Lloyd's. An undertaking is signed by a member not to exceed his premium limit (♦**premium limit undertaking**♦). The limit is allocated to syndicates in proportions agreed between the member and his members' agent.

Figure 7.5: Lloyd's chain of security

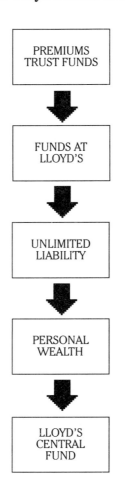

PREMIUMS TRUST FUNDS

FUNDS AT LLOYD'S

UNLIMITED LIABILITY

PERSONAL WEALTH

LLOYD'S CENTRAL FUND

accepted by individual syndicates adheres to these limits stringently in order to protect both members and policyholders.

Lloyd's requirements relating to premium income monitoring are dealt with by the underwriting agents department. This involves ensuring that cases of actual and potential overwriting by Lloyd's syndicates are identified at the earliest stage possible and that appropriate action is instigated by the agencies concerned or, where necessary, by Lloyd's.

D2 THE SOLVENCY TEST

Sections 83(4) and (5) of the Insurance Companies Act 1982 require each and every underwriting member to submit to an ♦**annual solvency test**♦ which must be conducted by a qualified accountant approved by the Council of Lloyd's. The annual solvency test is a very searching test of solvency requiring underwriting members to show that their underwriting assets at Lloyd's are sufficient to meet their underwriting liabilities.

Should any underwriting members fail to reach the standard of solvency required, they must provide additional funds to the extent necessary, or cease underwriting. The regulations prescribing the basis upon which the solvency test is to be conducted are reviewed annually by the Council and have to meet with the approval of the Department of Trade and Industry.

For Lloyd's as a whole to be considered solvent every member must show sufficient assets. Thus a member with more than sufficient assets does not compensate for a member with insufficient assets.

D1C Premium income limits

The volume of business members may accept in any year is based on their funds at Lloyd's and their qualifying means. If the premium income of members should exceed their premium limits, they may have to provide further funds in proportion to the amount of overwriting. Premium income forms the link between the asset base of the Society and the risks assumed by its members. A system of premium limits at individual member and at syndicate level operates to maintain the necessary security ratios. It is therefore important to ensure that the premium income

In simple terms, the solvency test is an annual exercise to check that there are sufficient assets held in an easily accessible form to meet policyholders' valid claims.

An annual audit of underwriters' accounts was introduced by the Committee of Lloyd's as a voluntary safeguard as far back as 1908. Throughout the years and under ever-changing conditions, the annual audit has proved to be the foundation upon which the security afforded by a Lloyd's policy rests. The stringent basis upon which the Lloyd's solvency test is carried out each year is accepted for legislative and other purposes as constituting adequate evidence of the solvency of Lloyd's underwriters.

D3 STATUTORY STATEMENT OF BUSINESS/ GLOBAL ACCOUNTS

Lloyd's is required to file annually with the President of the Board of Trade a statement of business prepared pursuant to Section 86 of the Insurance Companies Act 1982. This statement is in a prescribed form and covers the underwriting results and the solvency position of the Lloyd's market as a whole. The filing of the statement is fundamental to the supervision of Lloyd's by the Department of Trade and Industry.

The statement itself opens with an explanation that the information set out will relate to three years of account. The three year accounting convention enables Lloyd's to hold underwriting accounts open for at least three years from the commencement of each underwriting year. This time lapse allows for outstanding liabilities to be more accurately determined, so that when an account is finally closed, it will be possible to make a fairer assessment of the actual underwriting profit or loss on that year than would be the case if the result had to be declared after twelve months.

E

THE SYNDICATE SYSTEM

The syndicate system developed from a practice which was fairly common in former times whereby an underwriter would 'write a line' on a policy on behalf of one or two acquaintances who might have lacked the time or skill to sit in person at Lloyd's. With the development of marine insurance as a profession came an increase in the number of those employing an underwriter to act for them.

In the 1840s, the Committee insisted that all whose names appeared on a Lloyd's policy, whether underwriting in person or through an agent, should be elected members of the Society. This was one of the first of many steps taken to strengthen Lloyd's policies whose security today is unparalleled.

Early syndicates were small and reflected the relatively modest amount of business available to the market in those days. The big underwriting syndicates of today are a direct result of Lloyd's great expansion in the last 90 years.

In spite of dire prediction to the contrary, the new non-marine risks of the 1880s proved very profitable and one or two enterprising men at Lloyd's found themselves underwriting for larger syndicates than had ever been seen before. The non-marine market rapidly expanded and, with premiums flowing from all parts of the world, Lloyd's underwriters were able to cover the increasing volume of business only by accepting an ever-growing number of names into their syndicates.

Each member may join in one or more syndicates. Each syndicate has its own professional underwriter and a staff who have the responsibility of accepting risks, fixing premium rates and authorising the payment of claims on behalf of the members in the syndicate.

Each member gives such underwriters authority to underwrite insurance risks for him and the underwriter may delegate this authority in certain circumstances. Such underwriters receive salaries and, often, a profit commission for their services. A syndicate is composed of members who have similarly authorised a particular underwriter.

Within each syndicate, each individual member takes a percentage commitment of the risks underwritten by the members of the syndicate. The liability of each member in the syndicate is several and not joint. In other words, every member is bound to each risk underwritten 'each for his own part and not one for another'.

Whilst in the early days of Lloyd's each underwriter underwrote his own risks, the development of syndicates resulted in the current practice of each member appointing an ◆**underwriting agent**◆ or agents. Each member must appoint a registered members' agent to act on his behalf, to which he will be required to delegate the administration of his affairs at Lloyd's. He will be required to delegate to registered managing agents the underwriting and management of his insurance business. The member himself may take no active role in the conduct of the insurance business underwritten on his behalf, his agents having both the authority and the obligation to act always in the best interests of the member.

F
APPROVAL OF UNDERWRITING AGENTS

Lloyd's underwriting agents, which must be partnerships or limited companies and not sole traders, act as the link between the syndicates and the names. Lloyd's underwriting agents are reviewed by Lloyd's before being added to the register of approved agents.

Underwriting agents fall into two categories, namely members' agents and managing agents; some perform both functions. The register specifies the category for which approval has been given. Applications for approval give full details of how the agency will be set up, its management and shareholders, together with information as to the experience and history of directors/partners and senior staff, the number of names who will be underwriting through the agent, if a members' agent, and details of syndicates to be managed in the case of managing agents.

At least two thirds of the partners or directors must be members of Lloyd's who underwrite through the agency and are principally occupied in the business of a managing agency (in the case of a managing agency) and the business of an underwriting agent or Lloyd's broker (in the case of members' agents).

F1 MEMBERS' AGENTS

A members' agent guides new names through the application process, undertakes the administration of the affairs of existing names, assists names to comply with various applicable rules and requirements relating to their Lloyd's affairs, advises a name as to the syndicates in which he should participate, places the member on syndicates (subject to the member's agreement) and acts as a liaison between the Corporation and the member.

An applicant is free to approach other agents to act for him if he so wishes, but the actual application for membership of Lloyd's must be handled by one agent. It is permissible to have more than one members' agent. In this case the name must appoint one of his agents (with its agreement) to be his ♦**co-ordinating agent**♦. A co-ordinating agent has various responsibilities, including ensuring that the allocation of the name's premium income limits to various syndicates does not exceed his overall premium limit and co-ordinating the timely submission to Lloyd's of various documents in connection with the name's Lloyd's affairs.

An application for membership may only be made through a registered members' agent, who will provide the candidate with the necessary forms and will guide the candidate through the application procedures. Applications may be made at any time during the year, but only those received prior to 31 August will allow a member to start underwriting on the following 1 January. All documentation in relation to membership for an underwriting year must be completed by the preceding 30 November. As part of this procedure, the candidate must attend a Rota Committee interview at Lloyd's, when a representative of the Council of Lloyd's will ensure that the candidate is fully aware of the requirements and risks involved in membership.

A candidate must be sponsored by two existing members of Lloyd's, one of whom must be a director/partner or employee of the proposed members' agent. The candidate's principal sponsor is required to demonstrate a sufficient knowledge of the candidate. A number of members' agents make it a practice to remunerate sponsors or other introducers. Such remuneration may be continuing and is required to be disclosed to the candidate. There is a non-refundable entrance fee payable to Lloyd's by 30 November in the year of application and thereafter an annual subscription (based on a member's allocated premium income limit) is charged by Lloyd's.

The agent is responsible for briefing the candidate on the full background and responsibilities of membership of Lloyd's, and he must assist the candidates in preparing their applications. Among the information which has to be provided to the candidate is:

► a full description of the agency and of Lloyd's;

► a summary of syndicates' past results;

► details of the business written by the syndicates that the candidate is proposing to join.

During the last stages of the application, the candidate has to confirm to Lloyd's that all the necessary information has been forthcoming from the agent, so that ~~the Committee of~~ Lloyd's can be satisfied that the agent has dealt with the application in the correct manner and made all the required disclosures to the applicant.

It is also a function of the members' agent to review the underwriting arrangements of each existing name every year in the light of the policies and performance of the various syndicates, to ensure an appropriate spread of risk and to consider any particular requirements of the name.

Each name signs a standard ◆**Members' Agent's Agreement**◆ with his members' agent which sets out the powers and duties of and the services to be provided by the agent. It also establishes the obligations of the name, and the level of remuneration which the name is to pay to the agent.

The members' agent is responsible for the administration of the name's special and personal reserve funds; investments are normally made at the request of the name. The members' agent appoints trustees of the premiums trust fund, who hold the name's personal reserves subject to the terms of the premiums trust deed.

F2 MANAGING AGENTS

Each syndicate at Lloyd's is managed by a managing agent. Some managing agents may be responsible for several syndicates of similar or different classes, each of which will have its own separate identity for administrative and accounting purposes.

The managing agent produces the annual accounts of the syndicates, reflecting profits or losses made.

Each managing agent has a standard ◆**Managing Agent's Agreement**◆ with each of the names participating on its managed syndicates. This sets out the powers and duties of and the services to be provided by the managing agent, and the obligations of the name.

Each managing agency also has a standard Agent's Agreement with each members' agent through which names participate on its managed syndicates.

The managing agent is responsible for the underwriting and appoints the underwriter of each of its managed syndicates.

It is a requirement for managing agents to supply underwriting figures to supporting members' agents on a quarterly basis, to give an indication of the progress of the particular year of account. These figures are the total cumulative amounts for premiums and claims for the years of account remaining open.

In each year of account, syndicate accounts are drawn up by the managing agent in repsect of the ◆**closed year**◆ of account and for the open years (normally two). The reinsurance to close the account will be agreed with the syndicate auditors who carry out the Lloyd's solvency test in accordance with annually reviewed regulations agreed between the Department of Trade and Industry and Lloyd's. Every name must pass this solvency test in order to continue underwriting.

The managing agent is responsible for ensuring that the amount of business written for a syndicate is within the premium income limits allocated by its members to that syndicate. If a name's total premium income for all his syndicates should exceed his premium income limit in any one year he can be required by Lloyd's to provide additional security or to reduce his underwriting commitment.

The syndicate accounting rules set out the manner in which managing agents are to report to names.

Each name on the syndicate is sent a copy of the audited accounts together with a statement of his personal account for the closed year, showing his profit or loss for that year. Managing agents are responsible for the distribution of the accounts, to their own direct names on their syndicate and to the members' agents of indirect names.

The managing agent appoints trustees of the premiums trust fund in accordance with the terms of the premiums trust deed.

SUMMARY

This chapter has covered a great deal of ground which reflects the importance of self-regulation at Lloyd's. In the next chapter we will cover more practical matters when we consider the role and responsibility of the Lloyd's underwriter.

7

GLOSSARY OF TERMS

Agency broker
A corporate body which carries on insurance broking business exclusively as agent for another insurance broker, termed the 'principal broker' who is a Lloyd's broker.

Annual solvency test
An annual test to ensure sufficiency of assets held at Lloyd's to meet future underwriting liabilities.

Central Fund
A fund established in 1926 to protect policyholders in case any member of Lloyd's fails to meet his underwriting liabilities.

Closed year
A year of account to which no further adjustments are to be made and final accounts or profits statements can be prepared. This can be done only after providing for all outstanding claims by way of reinsurance to close. At Lloyd's the closed year is usually the third year of account.

Co-ordinating agent
One of the member's underwriting agents (where the name underwrites through more than one members' agent) nominated by the member to co-ordinate certain of his underwriting affairs.

Insurance Brokers (Registration) Act 1977
An Act providing for the registration of individual insurance brokers and the listing of corporate bodies, and for regulating their professional standards.

Insurance Brokers Registration Council (IBRC)
The regulatory body set up under the Insurance Brokers (Registration) Act 1977.

Insurance broking account (IBA)
A bank account held by a broker which must be separately designated to receive monies arising from insurance transactions payable from or to clients or underwriters.

Managing Agent's Agreement
A contract, in a form prescribed by Lloyd's, between a member and his managing agent, which sets out the duties, powers and remuneration of the managing agent and the obligations of the member.

Members' Agent's Agreement
A contract, in a form prescribed by Lloyd's, between a member and his members' agent, which sets out the duties, powers and remuneration of the members' agent and obligations of the member.

Premium limit undertaking
An undertaking signed by a member not to exceed his premium limit.

Umbrella arrangement
An arrangement between a Lloyd's broker and a non-Lloyd's broker whereby the non-Lloyd's broker is permitted to use the name, LPSO number or pseudonym of the Lloyd's broker for placing insurance business with or on behalf of (in the case of syndicate reinsurance) underwriting members.

Underwriting agent
A registered underwriting agent is a firm or company permitted by the Council to act as an underwriting agency at Lloyd's. There are three different types of underwriting agency:

▶ managing agent;
▶ members' agent;
▶ an agent that combines both functions: normally described also as a managing agent.

1. Which body establishes bye-laws at Lloyd's?

    (a) Corporation of Lloyd's.
    (b) Members of Lloyd's.
    (c) Council of Lloyd's.
    (d) Department of Trade and Industry.

2. The Council of Lloyd's is composed of:

    (a) Lloyd's past chairmen together with Corporation staff;
    (b) working members only;
    (c) external and working members of Lloyd's together with nominated members;
    (d) external and nominated members only.

3. What is meant by divestment when used in relation to a Lloyd's underwriting agency?

    (a) The banning of Lloyd's brokers from having an interest in managing agencies, or *vice versa*.
    (b) The equal division of shares in an underwriting agency among the syndicate names.
    (c) The removal of any controlling interest held by an outside name in an agency.
    (d) The separation of members' and managing agencies.

4. A provision in the Lloyd's Brokers Bye-law states that Lloyd's brokers must:

    (a) not be unduly reliant on one insurance company or syndicate in the placing of business;
    (b) place a minimum percentage of business at Lloyd's;
    (c) place reinsurance business through a specialist reinsurance firm within its group;
    (d) deal only with one firm of non-Lloyd's brokers in placing direct motor business.

5.	IBAs are:

	(a)	insurance brokers' accounts;
	(b)	insurance broking accounts;
	(c)	individual brokers' accounts;
	(d)	insurance banking accounts.

6.	Which of the following statements is incorrect?

	(a)	All Lloyd's brokers accounts must be audited.
	(b)	Professional indemnity insurance is compulsory for all Lloyd's brokers.
	(c)	Lloyd's brokers' accounting records need only be kept and preserved where specified by the Companies Act 1985.
	(d)	Lloyd's brokers cannot appoint new directors without obtaining prior consent from the Council.

7.	Which one of the following courses of action will normally be required of any member who exceeds his overall premium limit?

	(a)	To provide further funds.
	(b)	To resign his membership.
	(c)	To pay an increased subscription.
	(d)	To withdraw from his special reserve fund.

8.	Which one of the following would not be accepted as part of a member's funds at Lloyd's?

	(a)	Short-dated government stock.
	(b)	Bank guarantee.
	(c)	Private company shares.
	(d)	Cash.

7

MULTIPLE CHOICE QUESTIONS

9.   Which one of the following correctly describes the purpose of the Lloyd's Central Fund?

   (a)   To provide financial support to a syndicate in bad years.
   (b)   To protect the financial interests of the Lloyd's policyholders.
   (c)   To help pay losses when members would otherwise exhaust their deposits.
   (d)   To pay the debts of insolvent Lloyd's brokers.

10.   Who employs the active underwriter?

   (a)   The names on the syndicate.
   (b)   Each members' agency with names on the syndicate.
   (c)   The Corporation of Lloyd's.
   (d)   The managing agent.

11.   The responsibility for the distribution of the audited syndicate accounts to the respective syndicate members falls to:

   (a)   the syndicate's underwriter;
   (b)   the syndicate's managing agent;
   (c)   the members' agents;
   (d)   the Corporation of Lloyd's.

12.   Which one of the following would you expect to conduct the day-to-day running of the syndicate and look after the appointment of the underwriter?

   (a)   A members' agent.
   (b)   The Corporation of Lloyd's.
   (c)   The Council of Lloyd's.
   (d)   A managing agent.

7
ANSWERS TO MULTIPLE CHOICE QUESTIONS

1. Answer (c), Council of Lloyd's.

2. Answer (c), external and working members of Lloyd's together with nominated members.

3. Answer (a), the banning of Lloyd's brokers from having an interest in managing agencies, or *vice versa*.

4. Answer (a), not be unduly reliant on one insurance company or syndicate in the placing of business.

5. Answer (b), insurance broking accounts.

6. Answer (c) is incorrect.

7. Answer (a), to provide further funds.

8. Answer (c), private company shares.

9. Answer (b), to protect the financial interests of the Lloyd's policyholders.

10. Answer (d), the managing agent.

11. Answer (b), the syndicate's managing agent.

12. Answer (d), a managing agent.

UNDERWRITING; MARKET ASSOCIATIONS

A   Underwriting at Lloyd's

B   Market associations

INTRODUCTION

In this chapter we will consider the role and responsibility of the Lloyd's underwriter to his names, his agency and to the Society of Lloyd's and the role of the leading underwriter at Lloyd's.

The underwriter's duty to the Society of Lloyd's is at the same time both simple and complex. It is simple because honourable behaviour covers all that is required. It is complex because there are so many parties to whom a duty is owed.

We will conclude this chapter by considering the function of the market associations.

A

UNDERWRITING AT LLOYD'S

In this section we will consider the duties of the ♦ **active underwriter** ♦ at Lloyd's to his names, his agency and to his insureds.

A1   THE DUTIES OF THE ACTIVE UNDERWRITER AT LLOYD'S

Underwriting at Lloyd's Coffee House began as a purely personal business. Individuals accepted risks purely for their own personal accounts, backing their own judgment by risking their own fortunes. If the premiums they charged exceeded the claims arising, they retained the profit for themselves. When such an individual (or underwriter) was successful, it was attractive to both him and his friends that he should accept risks not only for himself but also for one or two of them as well, risking their money exactly as he was risking his own, and taking an agreed commission on any profit that he made for them.

LEARNING OBJECTIVES

After studying this chapter, you should be able to:

▷ identify the role and responsibility of the appointed underwriter of a syndicate to his names, his agency and the Society;

▷ list the duties of the active underwriter;

▷ discuss the particular responsibilities of the leading underwriter;

▷ outline the operation of leading underwriters' clauses;

▷ explain the function and purpose o market associations.

In this setting, the underwriter's duty is obvious and simple, and his fulfilment of that duty is virtually automatic. He is doing his very best for himself; his friends' interests are identical with his own, so he is doing his very best for them as well. His duty to behave honourably to his clients, the insured, is also self-interest, for without a reputation for fair dealing nobody would wish to trade with him.

The growth of the syndicate system at Lloyd's, the development of the agency system through to the separation of the members' agents and the managing agent's function leading to the active underwriter being employed by the managing agent (albeit as a director or partner) have all caused the active underwriter to be increasingly distanced from the individuals, his names, on whose behalf he accepts risks.

Q Having read thus far, to whom do you think an underwriter's principal duty lies?

A To his names.

The underwriter's paramount duty is to his names as it is the names' fortunes which are at risk and whilst no one can eliminate risk from insurance, which is a risk business, the underwriter must do all in his power to keep the risk of loss down to an acceptable level, both as to likelihood and quantum.

The underwriter has a duty to the principals in addition to common law duties as an agent and will have fiduciary duties and trustee duties.

The underwriter owes a duty to the Society of Lloyd's to behave honourably and similarly to all the many parties involved in the market, since Lloyd's prospers on its financial security and commercial integrity.

Despite the fact that, within the Society, individual syndicates are in competition with each other and broker competes with broker, with the Council governing the market place, all members of the market owe a duty to the whole. The Lloyd's underwriter is therefore not in the position of competing 'to the death' with fellow Lloyd's underwriters, but of competing on a basis which does not undermine the market's structure or reputation.

In carrying out his duties, the underwriter controls the insurance business of his syndicate. This can be broken down into various sections:

▶ **Underwriting policy**. The underwriter must determine the areas of business in which he wishes to be involved, and establish guidelines as to insurance conditions and premium rates. He must establish the size of lines he wishes to write, bearing in mind the syndicate's premium income and the nature and quality of the individual risk. He is responsible for ensuring that the amount of business accepted does not exceed his syndicate's premium limit.

▶ **Market disciplines**. The underwriter is responsible for his syndicate's compliance with Lloyd's regulations, market agreements, codes of conduct and market practice, both in relation to the business he accepts and in other areas of the conduct of business.

▶ **Records**. All syndicates must keep full and accurate records of the business they accept, and the underwriter must arrange for statistics to be created from those records to provide the necessary information for effective control of the account.

▶ **Reinsurance**. All syndicates need to be protected from catastrophic losses, and the underwriter must arrange and manage a reinsurance programme to give prudent protection at affordable cost.

▶ **Claims**. Although much of the responsibility for handling claims is delegated to the market claims office, the ultimate responsibility for claims matters rests with the underwriter, and he must always be satisfied that they are being dealt with to his satisfaction.

▶ **Market bodies**. The operation of the Lloyd's market relies very heavily on the co-operation of underwriters in various committees, working parties, etc. Underwriters are expected to play their part in supporting these bodies, particularly the respective underwriting association representing the underwriter's particular class of business.

▶ **♦Reinsurance to close♦**. The profit or loss of an underwriting ♦**year of account**♦ may not be struck until the account has run for 36 months. To do this a premium must be established to provide for claims, known and unknown, which still have to be paid. The evaluation of this risk is of paramount importance to the syndicate assuming the liability.

The reinsurance to close may include an allowance for ◆**incurred but not reported (IBNR)**◆

losses. IBNR losses are those losses that have occurred but have not yet been reported to the underwriter, i.e. they are unknown; for example, a disease which will eventually form the basis of an employers' or public liability claim but manifests itself many years later.

Figure 8.1: Duties of the active underwriter

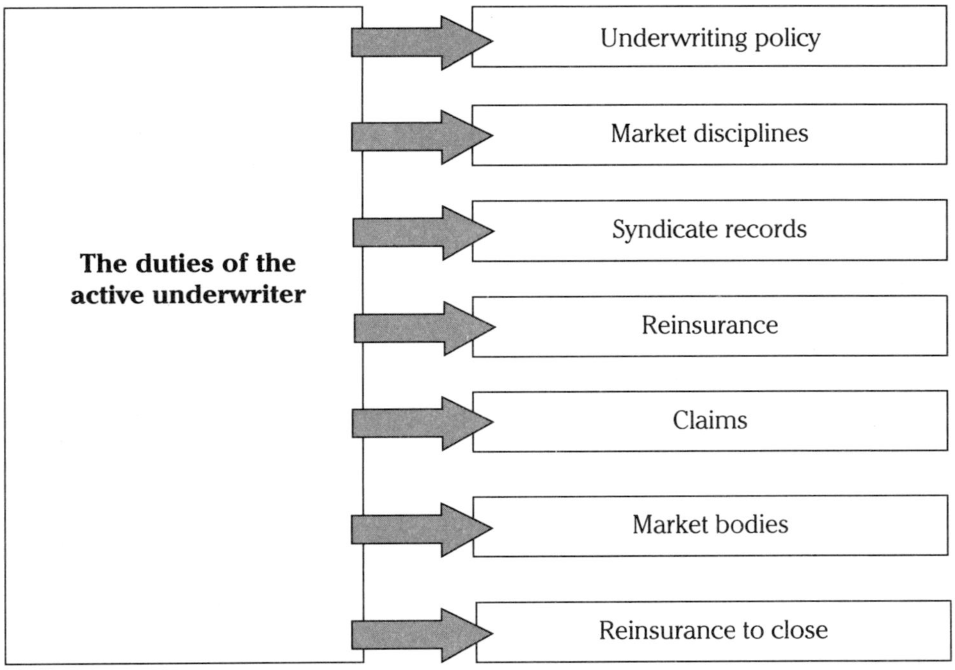

```
The duties of the          →    Underwriting policy
active underwriter         →    Market disciplines
                           →    Syndicate records
                           →    Reinsurance
                           →    Claims
                           →    Market bodies
                           →    Reinsurance to close
```

A2 DELEGATION TO UNDERWRITING STAFF

We have already studied the role and responsibility of the appointed underwriter of a syndicate. In carrying out his duties, the underwriter is supported by box staff, the size of which may vary from two or three to as many as twelve or more. However large or small, the essential functions of such staff are very much the same.

Before outlining the operation of the delegation of responsibility within an underwriting organisation, it is important to appreciate the vital importance of a system of delegation being disciplined and efficient:

▶ whilst the conduct of business at Lloyd's is, if not casual, certainly of an informal nature, nonetheless

a simple misjudgment can literally cost a fortune;

▶ if everyone involved in the underwriting for a syndicate follows one set of guidelines, any errors in those guidelines will become apparent and can be corrected. Without that discipline it is very hard to identify the cause of problems, yet alone correct them.

A2A Underwriting new business

Every underwriter has at least one person, in addition to himself, who actually underwrites new business at the box. In a small syndicate, it may be that only the deputy underwriter has been given this authority, and then only in the absence of the underwriter.

In large syndicates writing very broad accounts, there may be several assistant underwriters all underwriting full-time, usually each specialising in a particular class of business such as hull, excess of loss, treaty, etc.

More junior members of a box staff, not yet competent to underwrite new risks but having a sound understanding of the syndicate's business, may be authorised to agree, by initialling brokers' agreements, minor amendments to risks, declarations off covers and so on.

A2B Record keeping

One of the responsibilities of box staff is record keeping, including keeping records of all risks written, and the premiums received and claims paid thereunder, including sorting entries out into classes for the purpose of statistical analysis, whether it be by entry in books, coding items for computer operators to deal with or keying directly in at a terminal on the box.

Syndicate records are maintained for many purposes, regulatory and so on. However, the most important purpose is to enable underwriting staff to gauge the effectiveness of their underwriting and promptly make any necessary corrections. To this end it is the responsibility of all underwriting staff constantly to monitor the statistical records they keep and, where appropriate, to ensure that their colleagues are kept fully informed.

A3 UNDERWRITERS' REFERENCES

Wide variations of methods are used by different syndicates for their system of reference. However, the end objectives are the same. Let us consider an example of such a reference system.

A3A Purpose

The purpose of a system is to enable underwriters to:

► control the gross premium volume and the outwards reinsurance volume of the syndicate;

► distinguish between profitable and unprofitable business so that they can develop profitable lines of business, and either correct or cut back on unprofitable lines of business;

► control the aggregation of risk.

A3B Major divisions and individual references

A syndicate may be divided into major divisions. Each division should be carefully budgeted. Each division then contains individual references.

The purpose of the individual references is to enable the underwriter to:

► control the volume of individual sections of the major division;

► distinguish between profitable and unprofitable sections of the major division.

A3C Usage

When an underwriter inserts his reference it must not exceed twelve characters and any blank spaces before or in the middle of a reference should be completed using the digits X or O or any other digit acceptable to the syndicate. The reference is written in the space provided in the ♦**syndicate stamp**♦ which the underwriter uses on the original slip.

A4 THE LEADING UNDERWRITER WITHIN LLOYD'S

For the great majority of its marine, non-marine and aviation business, Lloyd's relies on the **subscription system**; that is to say, a single insurance is shared amongst a group of syndicates, each taking a proportion of the risk in return for receiving a similar proportion of the premium (only occasionally will a syndicate underwrite 100% of a risk).

For such a system to work, it is necessary that all underwriters subscribing to one insurance give cover on identical terms and rate of premium. To achieve this, a broker obtaining insurance cover for his client must find a group of underwriters willing to accept a share of the insurance on the same terms, and those terms must be the best available. This could not be achieved by negotiating with each syndicate approached. Therefore, the system has evolved under which the broker obtains quotations from one or more underwriters whom he knows to be competitive in that class of business. Having found the most attractive quotation for his client, he will seek support for those terms from other underwriters.

A4A The leading underwriter

The underwriter whose quotation is accepted is known as the 'leading underwriter', or leader. The broker's ability to persuade sufficient underwriters to follow that lead depends very much on the confidence other underwriters have in the leader's knowledge, ability and method of conducting business. It is central to the whole Lloyd's system, therefore, that leaders in their actions should take account not only of the interests of their own syndicate, but also those of the syndicates which follow them. This is particularly important in respect of alterations to a risk agreed by the leader, as it is very difficult for a following underwriter to stand out against the majority who might accept an alteration.

Leading underwriters' responsibilities extend into the area of claims where, although each individual syndicate can legally agree or refuse to agree a claim, the influence of the leading syndicate is very great.

A4A1 Leading underwriters' clauses

Some insurances are subject to many amendments, additions or extensions during their currency and, unless there is some particular arrangement, all alterations have to be agreed by every underwriter subscribing to the slip. To ease the broker's workloads, devices known as **leading underwriters' clauses** are incorporated in many broker's slips. These take various forms, but all fulfil the same purpose of, subject to various restrictions, authorising the leader to agree alterations not only for his own syndicate, but also on behalf of the other syndicates on the slip. The most simple clauses permit the leader to agree

changes, whilst other clauses require the first two or three underwriters on the slip to agree before the following underwriters are bound, and some spell out in detail the leader's authority.

Whilst ♦ **leading underwriter's agreements** ♦ are necessary for speed and efficiency, it is very important that their convenience should not be abused. Different syndicates have different underwriting strategies and systems, different capacities and different reinsurance protections. It is therefore incumbent upon both leaders and brokers to ensure as far as humanly possible that leading underwriters' clauses are not used to bind following underwriters to agreements they might otherwise decline, and that following underwriters are always advised of any significant matters agreed on their behalf.

B

MARKET ASSOCIATIONS

In this final section of the chapter we will examine the various associations, including Lloyd's underwriting associations.

All four underwriting associations have a common purpose, namely to represent their members' interests. None of these associations either effects or underwrites business.

B1 LLOYD'S UNDERWRITERS' ASSOCIATION (LUA)

Lloyd's Underwriters' Association was formed in 1909 and acts officially for all marine underwriters at Lloyd's in all technical matters relating to their business.

The committee of the association meets regularly to discuss the underwriting and general administrative problems which affect the great variety of marine insurance. It frequently makes recommendations to all members of the association with a view to improving the efficiency and profitability of marine insurance. Also, the association keeps its members supplied with all pertinent information that is likely to have some bearing upon the underwriting of marine insurance at Lloyd's.

The association acts in close liaison with Lloyd's Insurance Brokers' Committee and the Institute of London Underwriters, and appoints Lloyd's representatives to serve on various joint committees which deliberate upon problems that are common both to the Lloyd's and company marine markets. It is also represented on the International Union of Marine Insurance.

B2 LLOYD'S UNDERWRITERS' NON-MARINE ASSOCIATION LTD (LUNMA OR NMA)

In 1910 what is now Lloyd's Underwriters' Non-Marine Association Ltd was formed 'with the object of meeting periodically to consider matters relating to fire and non-marine business at Lloyd's'. One of the chief functions of that association was then, and still is, to circulate information to non-marine underwriters relating to non-marine business throughout the world. It is not, however, the purpose of the association to involve itself in underwriting.

This divorce between the provision of information and interference in underwriting was, and is, essential for the maintenance in the Lloyd's market place of a free and independent non-marine market.

On a broader front, the association works closely with the Council and Committee of Lloyd's, enabling Lloyd's underwriters to transact non-marine business throughout the world.

Membership of the association comprises all the active underwriters at Lloyd's underwriting non-marine business and they elect a board.

There are a number of sub-committees which consider the problems of the non-marine market place and have, incidentally, produced over 1,000 standard policy forms and clauses for the convenience of the non-marine market.

It is important to emphasise that these forms are in no way mandatory and probably more business is done on underwriters' or brokers' private or tailor-made forms than on NMA standard forms.

B3 LLOYD'S MOTOR UNDERWRITERS' ASSOCIATION (LMUA)

The introduction of compulsory third party insurance in 1930 led directly to the formation of the Lloyd's Motor Underwriters' Association in June 1931.

The problem of compensating the victims of untraced and uninsured motorists was identified many years ago and the association played an important role in the formation of the Motor Insurers' Bureau.

By the nature of the risk it proved necessary for insurers and their relevant associations, including LMUA, to give consideration not simply to the requirements of UK legislation, but to make provision for meeting the requirements of compulsory insurance laws in overseas territories, particularly within Europe. Notable in this connection was the formation of the green card system, which facilitates cross-frontier traffic. The LMUA played a significant part in the continuing development of the system.

The Association has a considerable commitment to the Motor Insurance Repair Research Centre at Thatcham, Berkshire, which is jointly funded by the ABI and Lloyd's. The centre enjoys a worldwide reputation for its knowledge and expertise in the field of motor vehicle repairs and its influence with manufacturers in new model design.

Lloyd's motor syndicates operate under specific trading names and can, accordingly, be readily identified. Membership of LMUA comprises all Lloyd's syndicates transacting compulsory motor insurance in the UK and they elect a committee.

B4 LLOYD'S AVIATION UNDERWRITERS' ASSOCIATION (LAUA)

Lloyd's Aviation Underwriters' Association was formed in 1935 to represent the interests of the Lloyd's aviation market.

Membership comprises underwriters of any Lloyd's syndicate writing aviation business.

A committee acts on behalf of the members as a whole, keeping them informed and sometimes making recommendations designed to improve the efficiency of the market.

The business of aviation insurers, like that of the airline operators insured in the market, is international in character and, accordingly, in addition to the administrative and domestic issues dealt with by the Association's committee, much of its time is taken up in consideration of foreign legislation matters and development in the international conventions governing the liability of air carriers.

The Association publishes a book of policies and clauses commonly used in aviation business, including the standard forms.

B5 LLOYD'S UNDERWRITING AGENTS' ASSOCIATION (LUAA)

Lloyd's Underwriting Agents' Association was formed in 1960 to look after the interests of underwriting agents and to examine and report on matters which might be referred to it by the Chairman or Council of Lloyd's. The association has no regulatory power. (The responsibility for maintaining and approving the register of underwriting agents is vested in the Council of Lloyd's.) The association acts as a forum for its members and, when necessary, speaks collectively on their behalf. The association is represented on a number of standing and *ad hoc* committees and it liaises with the various departments of the Corporation of Lloyd's on matters affecting agents and the names for whom they are responsible.

B6 BRITISH INSURANCE AND INVESTMENT BROKERS' ASSOCIATION (BIIBA)

The British Insurance and Investment Brokers' Association was originally the British Insurance Brokers' Association (BIBA) until the name was changed to the present one in January 1988. BIBA had been formed from what had been known as the British Insurance Brokers' Council.

The decision to form the British Insurance Brokers' Council was taken earlier by the four former insurance broking associations (the Association of Insurance Brokers, the Corporation of Insurance Brokers, the Federation of Insurance Brokers, and Lloyd's Insurance Brokers' Association).

On 1 January 1978, the membership of the four associations was transferred to BIIBA and the old organisations dissolved to leave a single national body representing the interests of insurance brokers in the United Kingdom. The purpose was to ensure that, for the future, united action was taken on measures to protect and promote the interests of the British insurance broking industry and that a single representative body existed able to react to or express opinion on matters affecting the industry.

A principal aim of BIIBA is to raise the standards of insurance broking in the United Kingdom with the intention of ensuring that new enhanced means of protecting consumer interests are made effective.

B7 LLOYD'S INSURANCE BROKERS' COMMITTEE (LIBC)

The Lloyd's Insurance Brokers' Committee is an autonomous committee of BIIBA. It is the direct successor of Lloyd's Insurance Brokers' Association, which was formed in 1910.

In 1978 the committee of Lloyd's Insurance Brokers' Association became Lloyd's Insurance Brokers' Committee of BIBA. The interests of Lloyd's brokers remain in the hands of a committee of 16, elected by Lloyd's brokers themselves.

Early in 1988, BIBA was renamed BIIBA. While the LIBC is, in fact, one of the regional committees of BIIBA, in so far as matters affecting the interests of members of the Lloyd's Region of BIIBA (i.e. Lloyd's brokers) are concerned, it is autonomous. It therefore continues to represent Lloyd's brokers on, *inter alia*, all matters peculiar to their relationship in the Lloyd's community.

Through numerous technical sub-committees, the LIBC for Lloyd's brokers (and BIIBA for all member insurance brokers) provides a service on a very wide range of matters.

All firms of Lloyd's brokers are members of the Lloyd's Region of BIIBA.

Figure 8.2: Lloyd's market associations

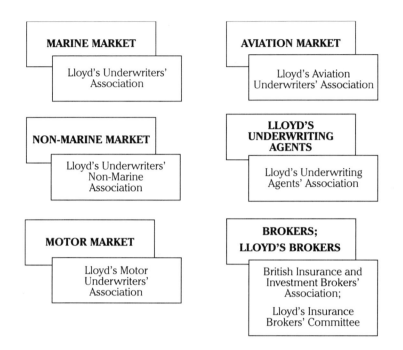

SUMMARY

The underwriter must establish guidelines for the business, comply with Lloyd's regulations and codes of conduct, keep accurate records, be satisfied that claims are dealt with effectively and arrange and manage a reinsurance programme to avoid ruinous losses.

Having looked at the position of the Lloyd's underwriter, in the following chapter we will consider the transaction of business at Lloyd's.

8

GLOSSARY OF TERMS

Active underwriter
The person employed by a managing agent with principal authority to accept risks on behalf of the members of a syndicate.

IBNR
A term used for claims arising from accidents or events which have occurred, but of which the syndicate has not been advised.

Leading underwriter's agreement
An agreement which allows for certain changes in conditions to be agreed by the leader without the agreement of all subscribing underwriters.

Reinsurance to close
The method by which the outstanding liability of a year of account is closed by reinsuring such liability, generally, to a later year of account, in consideration of the payment of a premium equal to the estimated value of known and unknown liabilities.

Syndicate stamp
A rubber stamp used by a Lloyd's underwriter. It incorporates the syndicate's pseudonym and number and is impressed on the broker's slip by the underwriter who inserts his line, reference and initial.

Year of account
The year to which a risk is allocated and to which all premiums and claims in respect of that risk are attributed. The year of account of a risk is determined by the calendar year in which it is first signed at LPSO. A year of account normally is closed by reinsurance at the end of 36 months.

8

MULTIPLE CHOICE QUESTIONS

1. The abbreviation 'TBA by L/U' is sometimes seen on a slip. This stands for:

   (a) to be arranged by all London underwriters;
   (b) to be arranged by all leading underwriters;
   (c) to be agreed by all London underwriters;
   (d) to be agreed by the leading underwriter.

2. Among the main duties of the active underwriter are the following:

   (a) to set the underwriting policy for the syndicate so as to best serve the names in the syndicate;
   (b) to recruit new names so as to expand the amount of business the syndicate can write;
   (c) to keep the amount of business written by the syndicate within the determined premium limit;
   (d) to evaluate the amount of reinsurance to close so as to cover any possible outstanding claims which will arise in subsequent years.

3. An underwriter's reference must not exceed how many characters?

   (a) Eight.
   (b) Ten.
   (c) Twelve.
   (d) Fourteen.

4. An underwriter's first responsibility is to:

   (a) the broker;
   (b) his managing agent;
   (c) his names;
   (d) the insured.

5. Which class of business is written by the LAUA?

   (a) Non-marine.
   (b) None.
   (c) Aviation.
   (d) Marine.

MULTIPLE CHOICE QUESTIONS

6. The LUNMA represents the underwriters in which of the following markets?

   (a)   Aviation.
   (b)   Non-marine. ☑ ✓
   (c)   Marine.
   (d)   Motor.

7. Lloyd's Underwriters' Association is composed of:

   (a)   aviation underwriters;
   (b)   marine underwriters; ☑ ✓
   (c)   non-marine underwriters;
   (d)   underwriters from all markets.

8. Which one of the following most accurately describes the role of the British Insurance and Investment Brokers' Association?

   (a)   To promote and protect the interests of brokers. ☑ ✓
   (b)   To deal with disciplinary proceedings against brokers.
   (c)   To represent brokers' interests at Lloyd's.
   (d)   To deal with the Lloyd's registration of brokers.

9. Which one of the following abbreviations stands for the Association respecting the interests of brokers?

   (a)   ABI.
   (b)   BIBC.
   (c)   IBRA.
   (d)   BIIBA. ☑ ✓

ANSWERS TO MULTIPLE CHOICE QUESTIONS APPEAR OVERLEAF

8
ANSWERS TO MULTIPLE CHOICE QUESTIONS

1.   Answer (d), to be agreed by the leading underwriter.

2.   Answer (b), to recruit new names so as to expand the amount of business the syndicate can write.

3.   Answer (c), twelve.

4.   Answer (c), his names.

5.   Answer (b), none of the market associations underwrite insurance business.

6.   Answer (b), non-marine.

7.   Answer (b), marine underwriters.

8.   Answer (a), to promote and protect the interests of brokers.

9.   Answer (d), BIIBA.

9

TRANSACTING BUSINESS; SLIPS; POLICIES; LPSO

A   Proposal forms

B   The slip

C   When an underwriter is on risk

D   Conducting business

E   Policies

F   Cover notes and certificates

G   Renewals and alterations

H   Lloyd's Policy Signing Office

I   Market agreements

LEARNING OBJECTIVES

After studying this chapter, you should be able to:

▷   identify the role of the proposal form and the main questions contained therein;

▷   discuss physical and moral hazard and the difference between them;

▷   outline the role of the standard slip and state the purposes of the main headings on the slip;

▷   identify situations when an underwriter is on risk;

▷   outline the other methods of conducting business at Lloyd's;

▷   illustrate the basic procedures for preparing a policy;

▷   summarise the role of LPSO;

▷   explain the importance of market agreements.

INTRODUCTION

The procedure and practices within the Lloyd's market are quite different from those of any other insurer. They are built on years of tradition, and still rely to a large extent on personal contact between those wishing to place insurance and those willing to carry the risk.

In this chapter we will consider proposal forms which are extensively used in the Lloyd's market for personal insurances. Perhaps more familiar is the standard slip, so-called from 1970 when the layout and headings on slips were standardised as an aid to accuracy and good practice. Policy forms may appear complex at first sight but they may be broken up into constituent parts. When the policy has been signed the next consideration would be any alterations, and then the renewal. The need to issue certificates of insurance and cover notes is considered in this chapter.

We look finally at the function of Lloyd's Policy Signing Office (LPSO) and market agreements. Thus in this chapter we will concentrate on the more practical aspects of how insurance is transacted at Lloyd's.

In figure 9.1 the triangular nature of an insurance transaction is shown:

Figure 9.1

At the apex of the triangle there is the risk, which could be the risk of theft, fire, incurring liability or personal injury. The insured, or proposer at the initial stage, is the person or organisation having insurance in force. The insurer is the underwriting syndicate which has contracted with the insured to provide insurance cover. The insured makes a proposal to the insurer via his broker, the insurer considers the risk and, if acceptable, determines the premium and the contract is evidenced by the policy signed on the underwriter's behalf.

PROPOSAL FORMS

♦**Proposal forms**♦ are used for obtaining information which an insurer requires before he can underwrite a risk. They are used in the Lloyd's market for household risks, motor insurance and personal accident risks amongst others, usually where the risk is small enough to allow one insurer to accept the risk in full.

Proposal forms are prepared questionnaires issued by the insurers, which ask questions about the subject matter of the insurance. Since the underwriter will use the information to assess the premium, the prospective insured should disclose all material information relating to the risk, whether or not specific questions request it in the form.

Proposal forms have the following functions:

► they provide underwriters with information about risks to be insured;
► the request a quotation of the premium; and,
► in some cases they describe the cover available from an underwriter's ♦**prospectus**♦.

A1 QUESTIONS ON PROPOSAL FORMS

The matters to which the questions on proposal forms relate can be sub-divided as follows:

The description of the proposer
Questions include the name, address, occupation and age for motor, personal accident and life assurance proposals. The address is a rating factor in motor insurance and may be so in theft insurance. The occupation is of particular importance in personal accident and motor insurances. (Excess because of age will be imposed for young drivers for motor insurance.)

The description of the subject matter of the risk
Underwriters seek knowledge of the risk proposed and ask certain detailed questions where they consider that the premium to be charged might be influenced by the answers given. The factors are termed ♦**physical hazard**♦. Physical hazards may also be checked by inspection. This frequently occurs in connection with an industrial risk.

Examples of physical hazards are as follows:

► The construction of a building for a fire risk, whether brick-built with a tiled roof or a wooden building with a bituminous felt roof.

► The type of premises concerned for a theft risk, whether a high risk as for a jewellery shop or a low risk as in the case of a baker's shop.

► The presence of dangerous chemicals in the workplace would be a high physical hazard, as would the absence of suitable guards on machinery, excessive noise or dust.

▶ In respect of motor insurance, physical hazard relates to the age and condition of the vehicle. The place where the car is normally garaged or used also has an impact on the physical hazard.

Amount of sum insured or limit of liability

This is the maximum amount payable under the policy and is also used by underwriters as the basis when calculating the premium to be charged. In the case of household cover, the basis would be the sum insured for contents or buildings.

Details of previous insurance history/character of the proposer

Questions ask whether the proposer has been insured before and, if so, on what terms and also whether an insurer has refused to renew a previous insurance or has increased the premium. Underwriters also ask for details of any present insurance of a similar nature. The underwriters ask whether or not there have been any previous claims.

The claims experience is of special importance to underwriters. If there have been many claims in the past then the underwriters will give special attention to the proposer before deciding upon acceptance or declinature and they may impose, in the event of acceptance, restrictive conditions.

Underwriters are concerned as to whether or not the proposer is strictly honest in his dealings with them and is careful regarding his property or employees. This is termed ◆**moral hazard**◆.

Underwriters may be able to form an opinion from the answers given. However, moral hazard is often difficult to ascertain and may not be apparent until a claim arises.

Examples of moral hazards include the following:

▶ Bad moral hazard: where the insured makes a fraudulent claim, deliberately destroys his property, or presents exaggerated claims.

▶ Poor moral hazard of an individual: carelessness resulting in many claims on insurers which could have been avoided by due care.

▶ Good moral hazard: the strictly honest insured who takes all steps to protect his property.

Period of insurance

The period of time over which the insurance is required and the commencement date are shown.

Declaration in proposal forms

On all proposal forms there is a ◆**declaration**◆ which the proposer signs and which declares that, to the best of his knowledge and belief, the answers the proposer has given are true and correct.

The following is a typical wording of a declaration as found on a proposal form:

DECLARATION To the best of my knowledge and belief the information provided in connection with this proposal, whether in my own hand or not, is true and I have not withheld any material facts. I understand that non-disclosure or misrepresentation of a material fact may entitle underwriters to void the insurance. (N.B. A material fact is one likely to influence acceptance or assessment of this proposal by underwriters: if you are in any doubt as to whether a fact is material or not you must disclose it in the space below.)

This proposal and the information provided in connection therewith contain statements upon which underwriters will rely in deciding to accept this Insurance.

I understand that the signing of this proposal does not bind me to complete or underwriters to accept this Insurance.

SIGNATURE OF PROPOSER   **DATE**

Q   In respect of proposal forms in general, can you think of some other important questions which could be asked?

A   Additional questions include details of the driver(s) on a motor proposal. Clearly, the underwriter will want to know who will be driving the car as this will influence the premium to be charged.

On a household proposal, a question could be asked concerning the physical protections at the house, i.e. whether any burglar alarms are fitted and details of the standard of door locks.

B

THE SLIP

Most insurance risks, except for motor and some personal insurances, are transacted by the physical attendance of the Lloyd's broker at an underwriter's box, requesting insurance cover. The written form of request is termed a 'slip' on which are set out the type of insurance, sum insured or limit of liability, period, location, clauses and conditions, as applicable, and most other essential details found in an insurance policy, such details being heavily abbreviated. Underwriters tend to specialise and market leaders emerge for certain risks. It is to one of these underwriters that a broker will go with his slip, seeking a 'lead' which is signified by the underwriter in question subscribing a proportion or percentage, termed a ◆**written line**◆, and signifying the various terms, conditions and rate of premium. Subsequent underwriters on the slip are bound to follow these terms and the premium.

B1 LEADING THE SLIP

Where it is necessary that a risk be spread among a number of syndicates, to prove acceptable to other subscribing underwriters the lead underwriter or leader must have the confidence of the other underwriters. To know which leader to approach first is an important part of the Lloyd's broker's expertise, although it does not follow that the first underwriter approached will necessarily lead to the slip.

Clearly, where large amounts are to be insured and many syndicates have to be involved, there is less opportunity for competition. For the smaller risk the broker may find a keener rate or better terms by shopping around. The lead underwriter is not necessarily the one who can write the biggest line, though normally he will write a substantial line. The broker then takes the slip around the market until the total amount or percentage required is subscribed or underwritten: the literal meaning of to subscribe or to underwrite.

B2 ACCEPTANCE OF RISK

The initialling of the slip by the underwriter is the acceptance of the insured's proposition. At the same time, he agrees that in due course LPSO will sign a policy on his behalf in accordance with the slip when the policy has been prepared and submitted by the broker. The signing of a policy may take place even after loss, and the underwriter cannot refuse to allow the policy to be signed on the grounds that the broker failed to tender it within a reasonable time after the initialling of the slip.

Such is the practice. The law is that, at Lloyd's, a contract of insurance binding on the underwriters to cover the risk in question is made when an underwriter initials the slip presented to him by a Lloyd's broker in the manner described and the slip contains an attachment date, i.e. a date at which the risk commences. Should a loss occur, underwriters subscribing to such a slip are in general terms bound to honour the lines they have subscribed, even though the broker has not completed his placing. When that slip is completed for 100% or any other required proportion of the risk with no amendment of the terms, cover is complete since those initialling have bound themselves to issue a policy under the terms demanded by the slip, if it contains an attachment date.

On occasions the slip, during the placing broker's passage round Lloyd's underwriting Room, may have changes made by successive underwriters from the original terms agreed by the leading underwriter. A following underwriter could insert amendments to the slip, which the leader and all preceding underwriters should be shown and agree by initialling these subsequent amendments. In the event that a broker is unable to obtain such agreement and is therefore unable to complete a slip on the amended terms, two slips on different terms, each covering part of the same risk, may have to be prepared by the broker for the respective underwriters.

Nevertheless, a slip containing an attachment date should not, generally speaking, be altered (except for minor corrections or clarifications) if the terms have been accepted by the insured, without the insured's prior consent.

In cases where 100% of the insurance is not subscribed and there is no other placing then the insured is his own insurer for the unplaced balance. In marine insurance this situation is covered by the Marine Insurance Act 1906, section 81, and elsewhere the policy conditions should take care of this position.

B3 THE NON-TREATY STANDARD SLIP (NON-MARINE)

The importance of the standard slip emerges from what has been stated above, namely that when initialled by an underwriter a contract of insurance comes into force between the insured and the syndicate(s) concerned.

Slips vary in minor details but, as an example, the main headings for a non-treaty standard slip for a non-marine risk will include the following:

Type   Whether fire only, fire plus additional perils (in which case those perils are detailed), public liability and so on.

Form   Here is stated which policy form is to be used with qualification or variation of perils if applicable.

Insured   Name, address and/or business and occupation is shown.

Period   The term of the insurance is stated.

Interest   This is a technical term meaning subject matter; for example, buildings, stock, machinery.

Sum insured   The limit of indemnity or limit of liability is shown.

Situation   The location of the risk or territorial limits is/are shown.

Conditions   Brokers will sometimes insert the special conditions they seek to have included, such as a small excess, while underwriters may impose conditions of their own before initialling the slip, such as the imposition of a much larger excess.

Premium   Sometimes, brokers will insert the rate they know the clients will accept: again, underwriters agree or amend accordingly.

Brokerage   This is usually expressed as a percentage of total gross premium by brokers and varied, or not, by underwriters, as the case may be.

Information   Here the broker should insert those material facts which he feels vital although his duty is fully to disclose all, often verbally, to the underwriters.

A completed non-marine slip for a non-treaty risk is included in appendix 1 to this chapter.

Slips are enclosed when documents are to be submitted to the Lloyd's Policy Signing Office (LPSO). Clearly, the correct compilation of the slip is vital since if the slip is wrong then the policy is wrong. The standard format of the slip is intended to assist not only the underwriter giving consideration to the risk, but also the policy drafter in the broker's office and those responsible for checking the policy and accounting for the premium at the LPSO.

Reference has been made to the 'information' section provided in the slip and to the broker's duty to disclose fully all material facts. The broker needs to be well briefed with additional facts and figures and must have available all relevant material such as survey reports, maps, plans, detailed claims records and any other documents or information which may have a bearing on the risk.

The broker is required to assemble a balanced and accurate representation of the risk and should anticipate, as far as possible, questions which are likely to arise. If, however, a question is asked to which the broker does not know the answer, it is his duty to say so and refer back for further information.

The need to disclose every material fact must always be borne in mind. Many a disputed claim has turned upon brokers' alleged failure to disclose adequately such matters as past claims experience, and this is an area of grave concern in the market.

B4 OFF-SLIPS

It is customary in the marine market for the broker to prepare a signing or ◆ **off-slip** ◆ from the original slip or open cover signed by the underwriters. The need for this procedure arises if, for instance, various options are expressed in the original slip or open cover, or if the original slip is for a whole fleet of vessels whereas separate signings are required for each vessel. The off-slip must be initialled by the leading Lloyd's and company underwriters.

In the non-marine market, if off-slips are used then agreement must be contained in the original slip. Similarly, the off-slip must be initialled by one or more of the leading underwriters.

C

WHEN AN UNDERWRITER IS ON RISK

This subject needs to be broken down into two phases. The first is the time of an underwriter's commitment to the contract of insurance, and the second is inception of cover under the contract.

Normally, an underwriter is committed to the contract at the moment he subscribes his line to the slip. In cases where slips are over-subscribed, and all lines are ◆ **signed down** ◆ pro rata, the final extent of an underwriter's commitment is not determined until the broker completes the placing operations and ceases to add lines to his slip.

Sometimes, for example when a broker is not certain that he has a firm order, a slip is placed 'Subject to acceptance, no risk', the letters 'SANR' or 'SANR Ldr' being written on the slip. Under these circumstances, underwriters are committed to the contract whilst the insured is not, and no risk attaches to underwriters until the insured confirms the order to his broker and the broker has so advised underwriters or, more usually, the leader.

The attachment of the contract itself is governed by its wording; it may be a specified date or it may be an event such as the sailing of a vessel, the birth of a thoroughbred foal or the launching of a satellite. The contract wording also defines the relationship between the period of the contract of insurance itself, and the timing of accidents for which it will respond. For example, a private motor car policy will respond for claims arising from accidents occurring during its currency (usually twelve months).

A products liability insurance, covering a manufacturer against liabilities arising out of faults in his products, may well respond for claims actually made against the manufacturer during the policy period, regardless of the date of his negligence or the discovery of the consequences of events which happened long before the inception date of the policy.

It should be noted that if an underwriter subscribes a line to a slip subsequent to the attachment date, and unknown to the insured or his broker, an event giving rise to a claim has already occurred, the underwriter is on risk and must pay the claim.

D

CONDUCTING BUSINESS

As we have seen, most insurance at Lloyd's is transacted by the attendance of a Lloyd's insurance broker upon an underwriter at his box requesting insurance cover, and the slip is the document used in these negotiations. In this section we will consider other methods whereby risks are accepted by Lloyd's underwriters. We will look at direct dealing, binding authorities and line slips.

D1 DIRECT DEALING AND SERVICE COMPANIES

Since 1965, an underwriter has been permitted to accept motor business (personal and commercial) direct from a non-Lloyd's intermediary, provided that a Lloyd's broker guarantees premiums due to the syndicate and service due to the assured from the non-Lloyd's intermediary.

This has enabled motor syndicates to compete most effectively with insurance companies for motor business which Lloyd's brokers found increasingly uneconomic to place in the usual way.

In 1990 (amended in 1991), the **Insurance Intermediaries Bye-law** extended these arrangements to personal lines business and commercial life.

The Bye-law also enables managing agents to set up special service companies to deal direct with the public for personal lines and commercial motor without any Lloyd's broker involvement. A service company is usually set up by one of the related syndicate(s), under a binding authority arranged by a Lloyd's broker.

D2 BINDING AUTHORITIES

The issuance of ◆**binding authorities**◆ is to facilitate the placing of business in the Lloyd's market. The system of granting binding authorities is particularly advantageous in dealing with small routine business both in the United Kingdom and overseas.

A binding authority involves underwriters granting some extent of underwriting authority to another party, known as the 'coverholder'. The coverholder may be entitled to issue Lloyd's certificates of insurance. Most, but not all, coverholders are insurance intermediaries.

It is up to parties involved to negotiate the terms of the binding authority as long as they conform to Lloyd's regulations.

A 'limited binding authority' allows the coverholder to issue documents evidencing that the risks have been accepted on behalf of underwriting members only after they have been accepted (and rated, if appropriate) by the leading underwriter as provided on the slip.

The coverholder must be approved in accordance with regulations made by the Correspondents and Binding Authority Committee and the binding authority must be registered (and, if renewed by the underwriters, re-registered) in respect of every coverholder authorised thereunder by the Correspondents Department.

D3 LINE SLIPS

This is a purely domestic facility within Lloyd's. As a Lloyd's broker often has a large number of risks to place which all contain similar characteristics, he will consider using a ◆**line slip**◆ facility in order to keep pace with the volume of incoming business, and to give a quick, efficient service to his client.

A line slip provides an established market of underwriters with which a Lloyd's broker may place either facultative insurance or reinsurance of the type specified on the slip agreement.

A line slip does not delegate underwriting powers to a third party, as does a binding authority, but involves delegation by other underwriters to the leader(s). The operation of the line slip allows the leading underwriter(s) to accept risks declared to them by the Lloyd's broker on behalf of all other underwriters who form the remainder of the line slip security. The following underwriters therefore agree to be bound by the terms quoted and agreed by the leader(s) for the amount of the line which they originally wrote on the line slip.

Once the line slip security has been established, the broker has a choice of whether to declare risks which he receives from clients to the line slip underwriters, or whether to place the risk individually with another group of insurers. Therefore, a broker is under no obligation to use the line slip market if he believes that he can achieve a better deal for his client by placing the risk elsewhere.

E

POLICIES

The proposer or potential insured has now made a proposal, normally via his broker, to the underwriter. When the underwriter accepts this proposal, terms have been agreed and the premium has been paid (or there is an agreement to pay the premium to the broker), then there is a contract.

E1 BROKER'S POLICY DEPARTMENT

Once the broker has placed the risk and issued the insured with a ♦ **cover note** ♦ (which contains brief details of the terms and ♦ **conditions** ♦ of insurance, the proportions underwritten, the subject matter of the insurance, the sum insured, the premium, the duration of the contract and the form of policy), the policy must be prepared in accordance with the terms agreed by the underwriter.

A broker normally will have a policy department, and a reinsurance broker will have a contract wording department. The purpose of both departments is to interpret and elaborate on the details and conditions contained in the placing slip.

The broker's responsibility is to construct the policy or contract wording from the clauses agreed by the parties in the original placement; the finished policy document being the legal document which may be necessary for the collection of a claim, particularly in respect of marine business.

Policy documents may also be prepared by the Lloyd's Policy Signing Office.

E2 SECTIONS OF THE POLICY

In the early days of Lloyd's, each individual policy would be prepared by hand and issued to the insured. As time passed, this became less practical and standard policy documents were pre-printed. These documents would have blank spaces where the individual details of an insured would be inserted (until January 1982 the SG marine policy form was in narrative form: this was the last remaining Lloyd's policy in the old style).

The narrative form of policy eventually gave way to the schedule policy.

 Q Suppose you were given a blank sheet of paper and asked to draw up a simple policy document, what would you include?

 A You would probably start with the class of insurance as a heading, then who is insured, what is the cover given, some conditions and finally a promise to pay your share of losses.

The answer above is an over-simplification but policies are divided into these sections.

E2A Recital clause

The section starts with the word 'Whereas' and recites the parties to the contract (and refers to the schedule for the name of the insured). It also states that the insured has paid the premium to underwriters.

The Lloyd's personal accident, life assurance and home insurance policies state that the insured has presented a proposal upon which the underwriters have determined their terms and conditions.

E2B Operative clause

The most important section of the policy is the section where the actual cover provided is outlined. Commencing with the words 'Now We the Underwriters' or 'We, Underwriting Members' in the latest policy forms, this clause sets out the protection granted to the insured and may be followed by exclusions to the policy.

E2C Schedule

The schedule is the area where the policy is made personal to the insured. Within this section are shown the variable details of the policy, for instance:

► insured's name;
► address;

- ▶ policy period;
- ▶ premium;
- ▶ details of the particular subject matter;
- ▶ territorial limits, if any;
- ▶ sum insured or limit of indemnity.

The policy schedule may be a separate document or may be incorporated within the policy form itself. The policy schedule assists in the checking of the variable information by the broker's policy department and the LPSO.

E2D Conditions

The policy form will contain certain conditions which will apply throughout the period of the policy.

Express conditions will appear in the policy form, whereas implied conditions which often relate to legal principles will not appear.

E2E Binding or attestation clause

This clause commences with the words 'Now know Ye' or 'The Underwriters' in the standard policy forms. The particular nature of Lloyd's and the syndicate system of individual liability require a wording which clarifies this uniqueness.

The wording of this clause makes clear that the underwriting members agree to meet only their share of liability shown in the policy.

E2F Signature

Lloyd's policies signed at LPSO are signed on behalf of underwriting members by the general manager of Lloyd's Policy Signing Office; a facsimile signature is used.

A list of syndicates showing the percentage of the risk underwritten (i.e., the ♦ **signed line** ♦ of each participating syndicate) is attached to the policy: termed the ♦ **table of definitive numbers** ♦.

The policy is embossed at the foot by Lloyd's Policy Signing Office.

E2G Exclusions

Exclusions can be particular, in the sense that they apply to a part of the cover provided by the policy, or general, as they apply to the whole contract.

In any policy there are normally a number of general exclusions which apply to all sections; for example, exclusions dealing with war risks and nuclear contamination risks.

E3 POLICY WORDINGS

A contract of insurance at Lloyd's is made between two parties, the insured and the underwriters (the underwriting members). The broker, as we have seen, is the intermediary acting on behalf of the insured to effect the insurance with the underwriters. The policy evidences the contract of insurance effected between the two parties and it sets the extent of the cover given by the underwriters. To do this, it must set out clearly and precisely the nature of the contract and contain all the terms, conditions, stipulations, limitations and warranties agreed at the time of placing the insurance.

Some important factors should be remembered by the broker when preparing the slip for non-marine business, etc.:

- ▶ The cover should exclude war and kindred risks as set out in the War and Civil War Exclusion Agreement.

- ▶ Underwriters have undertaken not to write certain financial guarantee business.

- ▶ Life cover can only be written by certain syndicates and is limited to short-term contracts.

- ▶ The insurance may require the attachment of a Radioactive Contamination Exclusion Clause, mandatory on all but a few classes of risk.

There are certain basic essential requirements to be expressed in the policy, namely:

- ▶ full name and address of the insured;
- ▶ consideration or premium for the contract;
- ▶ term or period of the insurance;

- amount of the insurance;
- the description of the property insured and the location and perils insured against.

E3A Policy standard forms

It is essential that whenever possible the policy is issued on the standard printed policy form. Within Lloyd's it is essential to know not only which standard forms are available for each class of business, but also the nature of the coverage afforded by them.

The policy of insurance does not need to be expressed in any special form, but long experience and custom has resulted in certain standard forms of basic wording being used and these are usually printed.

For non-marine business, the standard Lloyd's forms and clauses are prepared by the Lloyd's Underwriters' Non-Marine Association Ltd (NMA).

The variety of forms is extensive and provision is made for specific versions for use in overseas situations.

The NMA issues manuals containing all the forms and clauses. These are identified by title and by a reference number. The manual is divided into broad classes of insurance and the index enables forms or clauses to be found by title or reference number.

Forms and clauses approved by the NMA readily can be distinguished by the statement printed thereon that it is 'a form approved by the NMA'. Any other printed form or clause should not contain these words.

The procedure for aviation business is identical to that for non-marine, except that the authority for purely aviation forms and clauses is vested in the Lloyd's Aviation Underwriters' Association (LAUA) and a different printer's code number, prefixed by 'AV', is printed in the bottom left-hand corner of forms and clauses issued and approved by the LAUA.

It is accepted that no specific agreement is required from underwriters where insurances are written for non-marine or aviation business and forms and clauses approved by the NMA or LAUA are being used for the

purpose for which they were drafted. However, 'standard slip' rules require that, in the case of the policy forms used, a reference to it must appear in the appropriate position on the slip.

E3B Policy non-standard wordings

If a wording or form different from standard wordings or forms is required, reference must be made thereto on the slip. If the form is an underwriter's private printed form, then it may be used only for that underwriter. Unless that underwriter has a line on the slip, the printed wording must not be used for other underwriters without the express approval of the sponsoring underwriter.

The **Special Wordings Scheme** was introduced a number of years ago as a means of simplifying the checking of policies for certain risks for which special wordings are required. Special wordings may be required because there is no standard NMA or other market form or because a particular underwriter or broker wishes to use a special wording for the type of risk involved. Wordings within the scheme are usually sponsored by underwriters (although a few are sponsored by brokers or jointly by a particular broker and underwriter). Each wording is referenced 'LPO' or, since January 1984, 'LSW' with an identifying number.

Once a wording has been confirmed between the sponsor and LPSO as meeting the criteria of the scheme, copies are made available to the market from Lloyd's Policy Office (The Carlton Berry Co. Ltd). Each bears an LPSO 'logo' and its reference number. Wordings remain as first confirmed for an indefinite period unless amended by their sponsors. Brokers' or underwriters' private wordings which have not been brought into the special wordings scheme may be used provided the wording is specifically referred to in the slip and a copy of the wording agreed by underwriters is either attached to the slip or is on file for the broker at LPSO.

Certain non-standard wordings are registered by LPSO, and once registered there is no longer the necessity for underwriters to agree each wording and for LPSO to complete a word-for-word check on such wordings when applied to individual policies.

E3C Approved forms and wordings

The standard procedure is that all insurances placed are signed on approved forms, clauses and/or wordings. LPSO is required to see that this procedure is carried out and to obtain, through the broker, approval for any form, clause and/or wording (other than those approved by underwriters' associations, those of private underwriters, or those already registered by LPSO) from the underwriter(s) on the risk. The provision of basic forms and clauses does not itself complete the preparation of a policy of insurance and it is necessary for the person responsible for preparing the policy to have a good working knowledge of the type of insurance being dealt with, what conditions and provisions appear in the printed form, what these mean and what to do to modify or amend them to suit any special requirements of the risk being handled.

E4 MARINE FORMS AND INSTITUTE CLAUSES

The MAR marine policy form is updated by the addition of standard marine clauses.

Until 1 January 1981 the SG form was the only standard marine form in use in the London market. Its origins date back over 200 years to the coffee house days of Edward Lloyd and its original use was for wooden sailing vessels. It uses old-world phraseology which appeared in the first schedule of the Marine Insurance Act 1906 and which is adapted to meet modern-day requirements by the addition of overriding and complementary clauses. Each word has been tested in the courts and its meaning fully established.

The policy face may be divided into the following sections:

▶ **Assignment**. Whom the policy is in the name of and/or assigned to.

▶ **Duration of risk**. Tailored for a voyage beginning 'at and from' and ending '24 hours after vessel safely moored at anchor'. This section contains an implied seaworthiness warranty 'Good Ship' and customary calling provision permission 'to touch and stay at any ports or places whatsoever or wheresoever...' as long as the calling is reasonable and necessary.

This is followed by a space for the 'interest' to be identified:

▶ **Perils**. This includes marine perils (i.e. perils of the seas, etc.) and war perils. This section also includes a 'Sue and Labour Clause' and a 'Free of Capture and Seizure Clause', the latter clause being a war exclusion clause added in italics in 1898 in order to exclude war risks giving the underwriters the right to include or exclude war risks and charge extra premium if so desired. The Free of Capture and Seizure Clause excludes more war perils than are actually mentioned.

▶ Next is a space for the '**rate**' or '**premium**', the policy being in effect a receipt for the premium, and a 'Memorandum Clause' which states that small claims will not be paid in certain circumstances.

▶ **Attestation clause**. This is an agreement by underwriters to participate 'each for his own part' in the risk.

E4A The MAR form

The MAR form (MAR being 'marine') was introduced in 1982 following pressures to replace the former SG form by the United National Conference on Trade and Development (UNCTAD). The pressures to change revolved around the thought that:

> **...the immortalisation of an antiquated and obscurely worded document as being immune from any improvement is excessive and unnecessary and that consideration should be given to altering the method of granting (marine) insurance coverage from the 'enumeration of perils' method to an 'all risks' grant of coverage with specific exceptions.**

The MAR policy itself offers no coverage; cover must therefore be provided in the clauses attached to the policy which have been agreed on the original placement. The policy merely contains an attestation clause, a policy schedule which provides for details of the insurance and a statement 'subject to English Jurisdiction' on the face. It has been designed along with new clauses in precise, easily understandable language. The clauses used to expand/restrict the cover under the SG form should not be used with the MAR form and the clauses for use with the MAR form should not be used with the SG form.

E4B MAR policy clauses

The cargo clauses are termed (A), (B) and (C). All the cargo clauses follow the same format, the main sections being:

- risks covered;
- exclusions;
- duration;
- claims.

Clause (A) covers 'all risks' subject to certain exclusions, whereas clauses (B) and (C) are named perils clauses in that they name precisely what is and what is not covered.

E4C Institute War Clauses (Cargo)

The format of these clauses is similar to Cargo Clause (A). It states exactly what war perils are included whereas SG war clauses are used to include war perils excluded by the Free of Capture and Seizure Clause in the marine policy. Piracy is no longer a war peril but a marine peril.

E4D Institute Time and Voyage Clauses (Hulls)

The hull clauses also take basically the same format and are all named perils clauses, clearly setting out the perils and coverage provided.

Both hull and cargo clauses state English law and practice to prevail and they also include many of the elements previous contained in the SG policy form; for example, a Sue and Labour Clause has been included in the clauses.

E4E Other policy forms

In addition to the MAR forms there are a number of other policy forms in common use:

- ◆**Slip policy**◆ form. This is used where agreed (and in accordance with the slip policy scheme rules) if a full policy is not required to be issued. Many facultative reinsurances are signed on a slip policy.

- **'J' and 'J(a)' forms**. These are non-marine forms with a minimum of conditions so that appropriate wordings can be attached or used for marine business for various types of insurance for which the marine form is not appropriate; for example, marine liability risks.

- Some underwriters have their own private forms for use on certain classes of business, and insurance forms and clauses of other nationals are also frequently used.

E5 INTERPRETATION OF POLICIES

Words used in policies are given their ordinary meaning unless the words have a common business or trade meaning when they are so construed. Where words are defined by statutes then the meaning of that definition is used. Underwriters often define words or terms within the policy to avoid ambiguity. Added clauses take precedence over printed wordings where these are at variance with the same. Any ambiguity in wording is normally construed against the underwriters in favour of the insured.

In reading a policy there is a recognised procedure for alterations and attachments made to the same. This recognised procedure is as follows:

- handwritten wording takes precedence over all other;
- typewritten wording follows handwritten in order of precedence;
- rubber-stamped wording is next; followed by
- printed clauses; and
- clauses printed in the margin of the policy.

E6 ENDORSEMENTS

From time to time it is necessary to make alterations in the wording of a policy to take note of changes in sum insured, substitution of one item for another, etc. It would be costly and time-consuming to issue a new policy each time, so a sheet of paper, an ◆ **endorsement** ◆, is issued noting the alterations and any additional or return premiums involved.

The purpose of an endorsement is to give effect to an amendment or alteration in the terms of the insurance. Endorsements may be made by direct insertion in the wording of the policy document or by separate wording which is then affixed to the policy.

The word 'endorsement' may also be used in policies when certain clauses are only applicable if referred to in the schedule or subsequently endorsed on the policy.

F
COVER NOTES AND CERTIFICATES

The policy is evidence of the contract and contains all the details of cover, exceptions, conditions, period of cover, premiums and other relevant information. In certain cases, it is also necessary to issue further documents in connection with the cover afforded by the policy.

It is not always possible to issue a policy document as soon as the terms of the contract have been agreed. The practicalities of preparing the policy, checking and issuing the document take time.

In the meantime, there may be the need to prove that cover is in force. This is particularly true in the case of motor insurance where there is the legal requirement to have insurance. In this case, a temporary cover note is prepared by the motor syndicate or the broker and issued to the insured.

As mentioned previously, in the Lloyd's market brokers often will issue brokers' cover notes to the insured, in respect of the many classes of risk placed at Lloyd's, showing brief details of the terms, conditions and security of the policy so that the insured may be aware of the placement details.

Certificates of insurance are issued in respect of motor insurance to comply with the requirements of the Road Traffic Acts.

Where a marine insurance policy is lodged with a bank in connection with the negotiation of shipments overseas, a certificate of insurance is evidence to interested parties that insurance has been effected.

It is also compulsory for those who employ people to have an employers' liability policy. Once again, it is necessary to prove that there is a policy in force and the law requires that insurers issue a certificate and send this to insureds. The law states that the certificate must be displayed at all places of business, including outdoor sites.

Certificates are issued in connection with various other classes of insurance compulsory under statute.

F1 MOTOR INSURANCE DOCUMENTATION

Apart from proposal forms and policies, the main types of document used in motor insurance are as follows:

- ▶ temporary cover notes;
- ▶ certificates of motor insurance;
- ▶ green cards.

F1A Temporary cover notes

As mentioned previously, these are documents issued as evidence that insurance cover has been granted, pending issue of the policy.

There is usually a time limit of 15 or 30 days and the motor temporary cover note must include a ◆ **certificate of insurance** ◆ to comply with Road Traffic Acts 1988 and 1991 requirements. Brief details of the vehicle and the cover will be shown in the cover note.

Cover notes may also be issued in the event of a change of vehicle when a blanket certificate has not been issued or where there is some other major change in the insured's existing cover or a change in the class of use covered by the policy. Cover notes must show the time and date on which cover commences and must never be back-dated. The temporary cover note is superseded once the policy or an amendment thereto is issued.

F1B Motor insurance certificates

Q When insurance is compulsory in law, the law also requires that certificates of insurance are issued.

Why is this necessary?

A How else will the police or someone involved in an accident know that the driver has complied with the law and has a valid policy, short of all the drivers carrying the actual policy document with them at all times (which could be impractical due to its size). The alternative is to issue a small certificate of insurance.

Certificates of motor insurance are required by law to be issued as evidence that there is a policy of insurance in force covering the use of the vehicle on the road, as required by the Road Traffic Acts. The certificate of motor insurance is no more than evidence that the minimum cover required by law is in force and does not show that the insured has third party only, third party fire and theft, or comprehensive cover. A certificate may also be contained in a cover note, renewal notice or special document pending issue of the final certificate.

The certificate is divided into a number of sections describing the following:

▶ In the registration details of the vehicle insured. However, many motor syndicates issue 'blanket' certificates which state that the vehicle insured is any vehicle owned by the insured or hired to him under a hire purchase agreement. Syndicates adopt this wording so that a new certificate does not have to be issued each time the insured changes his car. The insured is warned by a notice on the certificate that he must notify underwriters of any change of vehicle as soon as reasonably possible after the change;

▶ the name of the insured;

▶ the period for which the certificate is effective;

▶ the persons or classes of persons who are insured to drive the vehicle in accordance with the relevant policy;

▶ the use to which the insured vehicle may be put in terms of the relevant policy and the uses which are specifically excluded.

There then follows an attestation to the effect that the policy to which the certificate relates is issued in conformity with the Road Traffic Acts of Great Britain and the corresponding legislation in Northern Ireland and the Channel Isles. Finally, the certificate is signed by an authorised representative of the syndicate.

F1C Motor insurance green cards

Green cards are used as evidence of minimum insurance cover in most of the countries of Western Europe and are instantly recognisable to the police and other authorities in European countries.

A British motorist who takes his car abroad is always well advised to carry a green card. This is so even though the 1972 EC Directive on the 'Insurance of Civil Liabilities Arising from the Use of Motor Vehicles' has theoretically made it unnecessary for motorists travelling abroad to have a green card as their policies are now automatically extended to provide the minimum cover required by the laws of the countries which have signed the relevant agreements.

It must be emphasised that a green card is simply proof that the minimum cover required by law is in force. It does not mean that the policy cover which the insured normally enjoys in the United Kingdom has been extended to apply in full to Europe. To obtain this extension the insured must specifically request it from his underwriters and pay the additional premium involved.

G
RENEWALS AND ALTERATIONS

Contracts at Lloyd's, with the exception of life assurance contracts, are generally annual contracts.

However, some risks are 'short period'; for instance, travel insurance and marine voyage contracts.

When a risk is renewed it is customary to approach the same underwriters and to negotiate with them again. If, however, the broker and the underwriters cannot agree then the broker will approach other underwriters in an effort to secure the terms he seeks, but he may need the leading underwriter's permission to do so.

If there is any material change in the risk while the policy is running, it is usually necessary to secure the agreement of the underwriters on the risk, and obligatory where the policy so provides.

G1 MOTOR RENEWAL PROCEDURES

Renewal procedures in motor insurance differ from those applied in other classes of insurance due to the existence of compulsory insurance and the need to issue a certificate of insurance. Because a certificate must be issued, renewal papers (including the certificate) must be drawn up a few weeks in advance of the actual renewal date. The broker passes the renewal notices received from underwriters to individual insureds.

Motor insurance renewal procedures differ from those in other classes because 'days of grace' are not allowed for the payment of motor renewal premiums. The premium must be paid on or before the due date or the cover expires on that date. However, there may be an unavoidable delay in the payment of the premium to the insurers (for example, the insured's remittance is delayed in the post) or for some other reason (for example, there is a change of vehicles just before renewal date, necessitating a change in policy conditions). Thus it is customary for insurers to print on the back of their motor renewal notice a 15-day cover note and temporary insurance certificate to ensure that the insured who intends to renew his policy and who has paid or is paying his renewal premium remains fully protected. Such temporary cover notes are not used in other classes of insurance. The cover note and temporary certificate give only third party cover to comply with the Road Traffic Act.

When the insured pays his premium to the underwriters he will receive a renewal receipt together with the certificate of insurance.

G2 DAYS OF GRACE

There may be occasions in respect of personal insurances where, although there was an intention to renew, the premium has not been paid by the renewal date. This could happen, for example, where the renewal papers have gone astray or the insured has overlooked the renewal. To cope with cases like these, underwriters include days of grace in respect of the home policy, for example.

Days of grace extend to 15 days after the renewal date during which time the insured can pay the premium. However, days of grace are not an extension of cover; they are 15 days, for example, into the next period of insurance. Once the premium is paid, the cover applies from the renewal date. Documents issued in connection with the renewal may be dated from the renewal date, not the day on which the premium was paid.

H

LLOYD'S POLICY SIGNING OFFICE

In the following sections we will consider the development of Lloyd's Policy Signing Office and its principal functions, the checking of documents and data entry.

H1 DEVELOPMENT OF LPSO

Policy signing at Lloyd's before World War I must have been a cumbersome and time-consuming business. The broker's clerk would prepare a policy and present it, with the slip, to the leading underwriter on the aforementioned slip. The underwriter's clerk would examine the policy and, if it were accurate, would impress the syndicate stamp and enter the line closed to the syndicate with the relevant reference and signature. It would then go into a basket at the end of the box, to be collected by the broker's boy on his next daily round, and then be taken to the box of the next syndicate on the slip. This process would have to be repeated as many times as there were syndicates on the slip.

One can readily imagine the condition into which a policy would deteriorate after weeks or months of being handled by brokers' boys rummaging through baskets and being checked and signed by a succession of clerks! An eminent historian described a Lloyd's policy as a 'bedraggled and disreputable document, a sorry advertisement for the greatest insurance market in the world'. With some syndicates signing up to 300 policies a day, the congestion and chaos in the Room with brokers' boys collecting and depositing policies and slips (many of which became separated) became virtually intolerable.

As early as 1910 some underwriters were suggesting the creation of an office for the signing of policies, but as with so many things it took the onset of war and wartime conditions actually to turn the idea into a positive reality. In October 1915 the Committee of Lloyd's approved the setting up of a signing bureau and on 1 July 1916 the Lloyd's Underwriters' Signing Bureau (LUSB) commenced work, albeit as a temporary measure to ease wartime conditions. Its use was purely voluntary and underwriters who so wished could continue to sign policies in the Room.

After the cessation of hostilities the signing bureau remained functioning and in 1921 the Corporation of Lloyd's took over its administration. The use of the bureau stayed voluntary until 1924, when it became compulsory for all Lloyd's policies with a sum insured of more than £100 to be signed through the Bureau. To give effect to this ruling of the Committee of Lloyd's, every Lloyd's policy form after 1 January 1924 was worded so as not to give the holder access to the funds or guarantees lodged by underwriters as security for their liabilities unless sealed by the Bureau (which, from 1 October 1927, became known as Lloyd's Policy Signing Office, although some people in the Lloyd's market still refer to it informally as 'the Bureau').

As may be expected, the demands on LPSO increased steadily over the years, with the original purpose of policy signing extended to embrace many other activities, such as the processing of treaty contract accounts. Mechanisation and, later, computerisation became necessary to maintain efficiency.

H2 PRINCIPAL FUNCTIONS OF LPSO

LPSO has the following principal functions within the operation of Lloyd's as an insurance market, namely to:

- check transactions and sign policies;
- extract and record entries;
- process ◆**syndicate reinsurances**◆;
- provide a central accounting system;
- provide statistical information;
- provide a special schemes service;
- provide technical services;
- control the allocation of identifying numbers and pseudonyms to both brokers and underwriters;
- develop methods whereby the quality and timeliness of Lloyd's insuring documentation can be improved;
- provide an LPSO London office.

To fulfil these functions, LPSO is split into Insurance Services, Technical Services and Documentation Development.

Insurance Services

Insurance services is involved with the technical and validity checks on documentation received from the market prior to input to the computer system, and is made up of the following:

- **Marine and aviation department,** handling direct insurance of hull, energy and related risks, direct insurance of cargo and related risks, and direct insurance and reinsurance (excluding proportional treaties) of aviation risks.

- **Non-marine department**, handling direct insurance of all EC and international work of a non-marine nature.

- **Reinsurance department**, handling all proportional treaty, incoming facultative and non-proportional reinsurance business, other than aviation.

- **Special schemes department**, handling claims (input of aviation and non-marine claims), records and amendments (processing of corrections) and syndicate reinsurances (processing outward reinsurance debit and credit notes).

Technical Services

Technical Services provides back-up to the checking departments, liaises with underwriters, brokers and other corporation departments, handles the upkeep of LPSO processing systems and the development of new Lloyd's systems and arranges for the production of statistics and procedure manuals. The LPSO London office is part of this department.

Documentation Development

Documentation Development develops methods whereby the quality and timeliness of Lloyd's insuring documentation can be improved.

H3 CHECKING OF DOCUMENTS

In this and the following two sections we will explain how premium work is handled under the three main LPSO operations (although not necessarily always in this order):

- ▶ document checking;
- ▶ data entry;
- ▶ numbering and policy signing.

The ◆**signing slip**◆, London premium advice note (Lpan) and, where necessary, a policy are deposited by the broker at the LPSO barrier in London. Throughout the day, the work is collected by the barrier staff and transported to the Chatham operating departments. The barrier is also used for the return of documents from LPSO to brokers.

Checking is not just a routine comparison of detail to ensure that documents are correct and that the policy truly reflects the agreement between the broker and the underwriter: it is also a monitoring function to confirm that the cover expressed conforms with public policy and the general law of the land as well as being possible in terms of the various Lloyd's regulations (for example, cover in the marine market will not be allowed for war risks on land). In cases of doubt the final decision as to whether a policy should be processed through to signing would lie with the appropriate Deputy Chairman of Lloyd's. For marine business, an off-slip is used in the majority of cases, initialled by the leading underwriter and containing

details of the risk. The original slip is more commonly used for non-marine business.

A London premium advice note (Lpan) has to be received (having been drawn up by the broker) for checking. In LPSO various codes have to be inserted in the Lpan, such as Department of Trade and Industry (DTI) classifications of business, audit, VAT and settlement currency.

Although it is the Lloyd's broker's responsibility to allocate the DTI code on the slip, this forms the basis of the very important LPSO function of producing statistics for the DTI both for balance of payments purposes and to meet the statutory requirement of giving the DTI an analysis of the collective annual premium of Lloyd's underwriters.

The submission to LPSO for checking can follow the ◆**separation procedure**◆ under which stage 1 is just the slip and the Lpan, followed by stage 2 when the slip comes back again with the policy documents. Alternatively, under 'S & A' (◆**signing and accounting**◆) everything required can be submitted simultaneously; namely, policy, Lpan and slip. Another facility is available (except for marine business) whereby brokers submit policies to LPSO for signing as soon as they are prepared: i.e. processed with a 'for declaration only' (FDO) Lpan to establish the year of account, without any commitment to settle the premium on a specific date which will be paid by additional premium (AP).

In the case of additional premiums (APs) and return premiums (RPs), the slip endorsement and policy endorsement will be checked. One of the most important tasks of the operating departments is to ensure that the receipt and payment of monies between brokers and underwriters is dealt with promptly.

War risks premiums have to be notified separately. LPSO (together with certain other bodies, such as the Institute of London Underwriters, with whom they operate a joint scheme) hold sets of agreed brokers' clauses which may apply to a case being processed.

H4 DATA ENTRY

The Lpan (see appendix 2) and broker's slip serve as keying documents for data entry. At this stage the

LPSO signing number and date have not been allocated.

Each case, now with an ID number (such as 6522521), proceeds from the checkers to data entry. The ID will be employed until the policy is numbered and the system has a 'fail-safe', whereby no item that is subject to a query can be numbered until the query is resolved. ID numbers are held in the system for a maximum of three months, although most cases in fact see the policy number affixed the same day.

The system checks that the Lpan and the slip match, that the currency quoted is valid, and that the lines and the pseudonyms are correct.

Narrative (in effect, a precis of the policy details), which may have been written onto the Lpan by the checker or will be created from details keyed at the data entry stage, will eventually appear on the advice despatched to underwriters after processing.

Work within the system is given priority by the sequence of presentation dates (i.e. dates of presentation at the LPSO barrier).

A very high priority is given to security in the data entry area. The operator has a secret password which is changed quarterly. A trainee may enter data, but only an accredited operator can clear the data. Similarly, only senior personnel can clear certain items which are in some way out of the ordinary, such as foreign codes or old exchange rates.

Once all the data has been entered into a series of input screens and validated by the system, the documents can be numbered if error-free.

H5 NUMBERING AND POLICY SIGNING

The last stage in the process is the signing function, which incorporates policy numbering. It is interesting to note that the same numbers are used each day: it is the date that changes, thus every working morning the signing area starts from 001 and goes up in batches of 100.

After successful data entry, the work can be numbered so that no documents are delayed, awaiting attention. The signing number and date is applied to all documents. The LPSO number and key fields are input from the Lpan into the system on a VDU by recalling and validating against the original system entry. The transaction can then be released for accounting processing.

The work is stored overnight and checked against an audit report on the following day. The Lpans are separated from the brokers' documents and will eventually be microfilmed. Schedules, showing the syndicates, lines and references, and produced from the data keyed at the data entry stage, are checked and attached to the policy (see appendix 3).

After attachment of schedules, the policy is signed in the name of the current general manager of LPSO and the signing number and date is inserted. The original policy will receive the Lloyd's embossment (stickers are affixed to copies) and then documents are sent to London for collection by the brokers. Periodically, brokers have to trace urgently required documents that are in the course of LPSO processing. LPSO has a 'search procedure' which can be used as soon as an enquiry is received so as to locate documents with the minimum of delay.

The workflow diagram, opposite, shows the progress of work through LPSO.

Figure 9.2: Diagrammatic workflow for a premium transaction

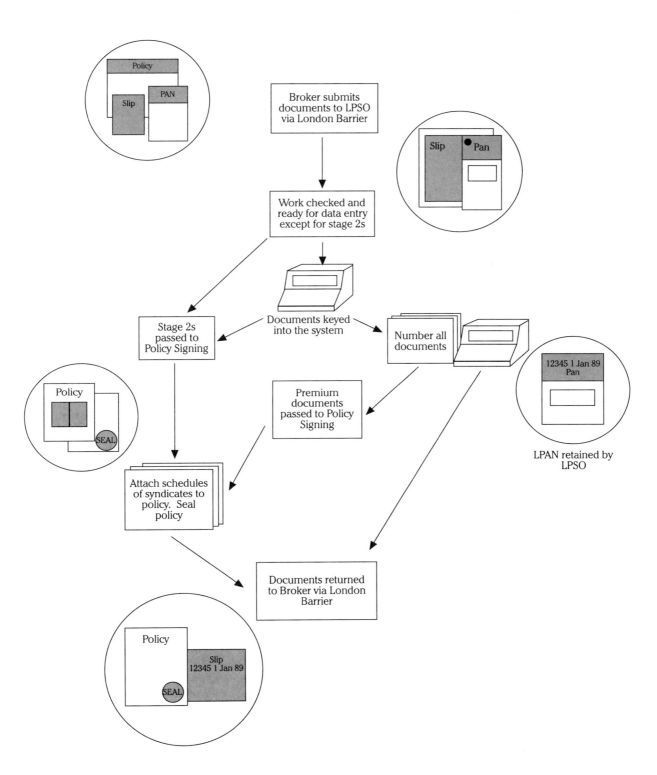

H6 BROKER'S LPSO NUMBER AND PSEUDONYM

A broker's LPSO number and pseudonym are allocated to each Lloyd's broker by the Technical Services Department, LPSO Chatham, for identification, validation and accounting purposes.

A broker's LPSO number consists of three digits and the pseudonym of two or three letters. The LPSO number and pseudonum have the purposes of acting as an identification for all accounting between the broker and underwriters within the Lloyd's central accounting and as a unique identification and reference for each broker. Thus they enable the LPSO to check the validity of the broker's entries being processed and allow for quick and accurate sorting of documents at the LPSO reception barrier for return to the relevant broker. The broker's LPSO number and pseudonym must be shown accurately on every document submitted to LPSO, as failure to do this will cause delay.

Certain broking organisations are allocated several LPSO numbers and pseudonyms and it is essential that the same number and pseudonym be used on all documents relating to the one item.

H7 SYNDICATE PSEUDONYMS

Each Lloyd's syndicate is issued with a unique number by which that syndicate is identified. This number is used for all Lloyd's accounting purposes.

When an underwriter subscribes a line to a slip, he adds an initial as authority and his syndicate number to identify the syndicate, and this is transferred onto all documentary and computer entries. As it is essential to avoid errors in copying or keying in these numbers, each syndicate is also given a unique three letter pseudonym for use in addition to the syndicate number. Lloyd's central accounting computers are programmed to reject any entries where the number and the pseudonym are not compatible, making it almost impossible for an entry to be processed to the wrong syndicate.

H8 THE CENTRAL ACCOUNTING SYSTEM

Prior to the introduction of central accounting, each broker and each syndicate maintained an account in respect of their mutual transactions. These accounts were agreed and settled periodically. However, even when business at Lloyd's was at a volume far lower than it is today, the amount of work (particularly having regard to the differing currencies and consequent different rates of exchange) must have been substantial and for brokers and underwriters employed many staff just agreeing and reconciling accounts.

The idea of a central accounting system was considered quite seriously as early as 1914. However, the scheme, administered by LPSO, did not come into operation until 1961. Clearly, modern technology, and especially computerisation, played and still plays a very large role in enabling the central accounting system to function smoothly. Accounting information supplied by the brokers on Lpans and other documents (such as claim/refund forms) can be checked at LPSO and then entered into the computer.

By way of the central accounting system, a broker no longer has to keep a separate account for each syndicate: instead, only one account need be maintained with Lloyd's syndicates through Lloyd's central accounting. This account embraces three settlement currencies only (sterling, US dollars and Canadian dollars) and all other currencies must be exchanged to one of these three.

Sterling settlements are handled by Lloyd's Central Accounting Office in London in accordance with fixed settlement dates outlined in the Central Accounting Calendar. US dollar and Canadian dollar settlements are arranged by the Lloyd's American and Canadian Trust Fund Office in London rather than through the Central Accounting Office.

Crediting and debiting of US dollar balances on the appropriate calendar dates is done by Citibank NA in London and a similar function for Canadian dollar balances is carried out by the Royal Bank of Canada in Montreal.

The accounting information keyed to LPSO produces advices for brokers and underwriters. All advices bear the Central Accounting Tabulation reference. The advices from central accounting are underwriter tabulations for underwriters (see appendix 4) and broker daily statements for brokers (see appendix 5).

These list transactions processed by LPSO with the monetary amounts sub-totalled by payment date on cash tabulations. (Underwriters have the option to dispense with their tabulations.)

Networked data is also available to brokers and underwriters if they are connected to the London Insurance Market Network (LIMNET) and the Information Centre (IC) service. Brokers' and underwriters' accounting information can be determined from the electronic message transmitted daily.

Underwriters receive the Underwriter Signing Message (USM) and brokers may receive the Bureaux Signing Message (BSM).

For settlement purposes, underwriters and brokers receive settlement statements (see appendix 6) and settlement listings which are available to the market each Wednesday, detailing the amounts due for settlement on the following Friday.

Settlement statements list the total cash balances due for payment which have previously been shown on the brokers' daily statements and underwriters' tabulations. To compliment the statements, the settlement listings detail the amounts to be paid or received at broker/syndicate number and/or controlling group broker/syndicate number level.

UK motor business and some overseas motor business are excluded from the central accounting scheme.

H9 TERMS OF CREDIT AND TERMS OF TRADE SCHEMES

One of the market practices at Lloyd's is that the broker initiates the central accounting 'billing' procedure by having an entry 'taken down' by LPSO. This is unlike most commercial organisations, where the supplier of services normally initiates the charging procedure and follows up the collection of debts.

The original 'terms of credit scheme' was developed during the 1970s under which, when each risk is accepted by underwriters, an agreed period of credit is negotiated, within overall limits which have been determined for each type of risk, country and currency, within which brokers can expect to account to underwriters for the premium. The scheme still applies to aviation risks.

The terms of trade scheme' was introduced in January 1987 and replaces the terms of credit scheme for the non-marine market. The recommended terms are markers which underwriters and brokers have agreed can reasonably be achieved in most cases for most of the time. The terms for each risk are negotiable in individual cases between individual underwriters and brokers as part of the rating process.

The marine terms of trade scheme adopted from 1 January 1992 is very similar but has some major differences. For example, the periods given are still maximums rather than recommended periods.

H9A Late settlement reporting system

Having determined an agreed period of credit, the settlement performance of a broker is measured by comparing the settlement due date with the date that documentation is presented to LPSO by the broker, rather than actual payment dates.

The late settlement reporting system reports broker's performances:

▶ in relation to individual syndicates;
▶ in each market;
▶ overall.

Also, details of all items signed late are given to brokers to assist in their review and control of late signings.

The statistics show the proportion of premiums settled late compared with the total premiums included in the scheme.

The then Committee of Lloyd's set up the Late Settlement Review Committee to review brokers who settle late, with the power to take action against brokers who it feels are persistently offending without good reason. This committee is made up of representatives from the market associations and LIBC.

I
MARKET AGREEMENTS

There are a number of different ◆**market agreements**◆ entered into by Lloyd's underwriters and/or insurance companies, whereby underwriters undertake to adhere to a specific course of action or understanding. The agreements are generally intended to facilitate the processing of business or maintain the solvency of underwriters. They may also arise from national or international legislative requirements. There are many agreements covering a number of subjects. These can be divided into 'market-wide' agreements and 'single market' agreements.

Market-wide agreements are entered into by both Lloyd's underwriters and insurance companies; for example, the ◆**War and Civil War Risks Exclusion Agreement**◆ between Lloyd's and BIA (now ABI: Association of British Insurers), which was brought into effect in 1937 and re-issued on 1 April 1982, following a major revision. The current agreement provides that underwriters will exclude loss, damage or liabilities resulting directly or indirectly from war and civil war from all insurances and reinsurances other than those excepted classes listed in the agreement. The list of excepted classes to which the agreement does not extend includes, for example, life and personal accident and professional indemnity insurances. War and civil war may be included in marine hull policies, subject to the terms of the War Risk on Hulls Agreement, in marine cargo policies, subject to the terms of the ◆**War Risk Waterborne Agreement**◆.

Boards set up by Lloyd's and the insurance companies deal with questions arising out of the agreements and applications to amend the list of excepted classes.

I1 SINGLE MARKET AGREEMENTS

Agreements limited to a single market extend across only a single market, that is, marine, aviation, or non-marine. They may be joint agreements between Lloyd's underwriters and insurance companies. Examples of such agreements include the use of leading underwriters' clauses in all three markets, the 'companies collective signing agreement' (CCSA) (non-marine), and the marine Waterborne Agreement (which reinforces the war and civil war exclusion agreement insofar as cargo business is concerned).

The original Leading Underwriter's Agreement (NMA) was introduced in 1936 and revised in 1965 to facilitate the handling of changes in individual insurances without the need for the broker to see all underwriters subscribing to a risk. The Agreement lays down four categories of matters which must be shown to all underwriters and provides (with certain reservations) that all other matters need only to be seen by the two leading Lloyd's underwriters. This agreement was drawn up and is administered by the Lloyd's Underwriters' Non-Marine Association.

The CCSA (non-marine) was introduced in 1965 and a large number of insurance companies in the London market participate. It authorises the leading CCSA company to sign a collective policy on behalf of all other CCSA companies on the risk, thus considerably reducing the number of signatures needed. The agreement provides an indemnity to the leading company against any liability incurred as signatory which would not otherwise have been incurred if the policy had been individually signed by all companies. In addition, a number of schemes have been introduced by Lloyd's underwriters aimed at facilitating the processing of business at Lloyd's and these have required market agreements to authorise their operation. Examples include schemes to simplify the processing of non-marine claims, small claims, small additional premiums and return premiums, and treaty balances.

SUMMARY

We have considered the transaction of business from the proposal to the preparation of the policy, including any alterations, through to renewal of the business. In the next chapter we will consider the transfer of premiums and the settlement of claims.

APPENDIX 1: SPECIMEN NON-MARINE SLIP

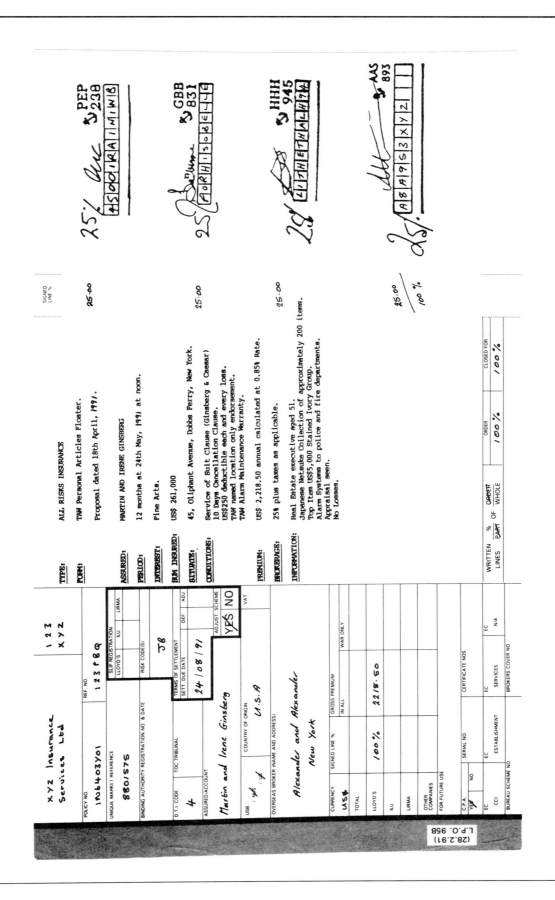

APPENDIX 2: LONDON PREMIUM ADVICE NOTE

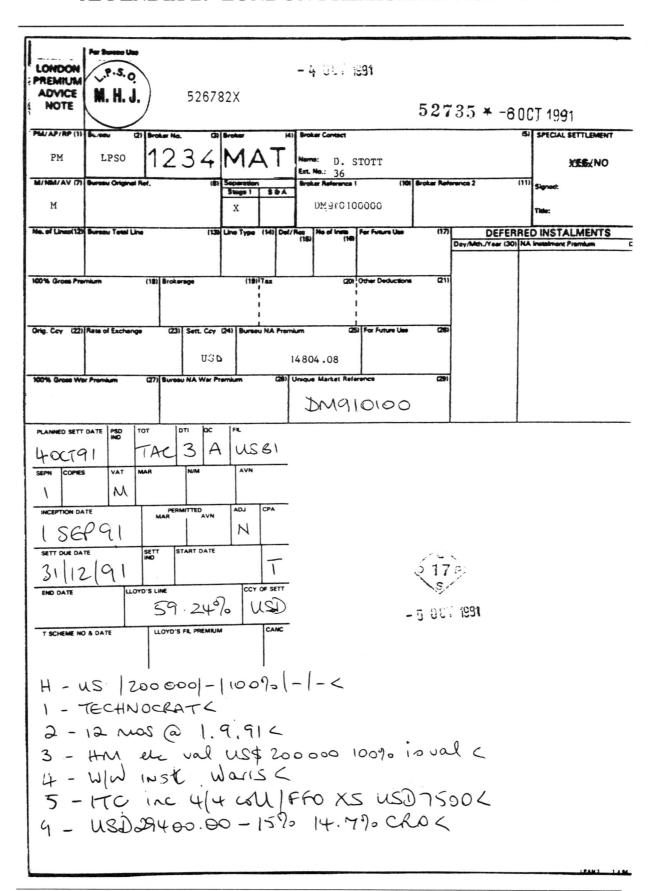

LONDON PREMIUM ADVICE NOTE

For Bureau Use
L.P.S.O.
M.H.J.

526782X

- 4 OCT 1991

52735 * -8 OCT 1991

PM/AP/RP (1)	Bureau (2)	Broker No. (3)	Broker (4)	Broker Contact	(5) SPECIAL SETTLEMENT
PM	LPSO	1234	MAT	Name: D. STOTT Ext. No.: 36	~~YES~~/NO

M/NM/AV (7)	Bureau Original Ref. (8)	Separation		Broker Reference 1 (10)	Broker Reference 2 (11)	Signed:
		Stage 1	S & A			
M		X		DM910100000		Title:

No. of Lines (12)	Bureau Total Line (13)	Line Type (14)	Def/Res (15)	No of Insts (16)	For Future Use (17)	DEFERRED INSTALMENTS
						Day/Mth./Year (30) NA Instalment Premium

100% Gross Premium (18)	Brokerage (19)	Tax (20)	Other Deductions (21)

Orig. Ccy (22)	Rate of Exchange (23)	Sett. Ccy (24)	Bureau NA Premium (25)	For Future Use (26)
		USD	14804.08	

100% Gross War Premium (27)	Bureau NA War Premium (28)	Unique Market Reference (29)
		DM910100

PLANNED SETT DATE	PSD IND	TOT	DTI	QC	FIL
4 OCT 91		TAC	3	A	US81

SEPN	COPIES	VAT	MAR	N/M	AVN
1		M			

INCEPTION DATE	PERMITTED		ADJ	CPA
	MAR	AVN		
1 SEP 91			N	

SETT DUE DATE	SETT IND	START DATE	
31/12/91			T

END DATE	LLOYD'S LINE	CCY OF SETT
	59.24%	USD

0 17 0
S
- 9 OCT 1991

T SCHEME NO & DATE	LLOYD'S FIL PREMIUM	CANC

H - US | 200 000| - |100%| - | - <
1 - TECHNOCRAT<
2 - 12 MOS @ 1.9.91<
3 - HM etc val US$ 200 000 100% is val <
4 - W/W inst. Waris <
5 - ITC inc 4/4 coll/FFO XS USD 7500<
9 - USD 29400.00 - 15% 14.7% CRO<

LPAN 1 14 M

APPENDIX 3: SIGNING SCHEDULE

Definitive numbers of the Syndicates and proportions

The Lines signed hereunder are percentages of the total amount insured and not of the amount of this policy.

FOR LPSO USE ONLY	BROKER	LPSO NO. & DATE		
CPD33R 2502 1462	123	52735	8 10 91	

AMOUNT, PERCENTAGE OR PROPORTION	SYNDICATE	UNDERWRITER'S REF.	PAGE
			1
PERCENT			
14.22	855	T73F88N01472	
9.43	287	AL78688AX843	
4.74	18	3212X544401N	
4.74	1091	TJ7F88G00184	
4.74	804	O7A05Y88	
4.74	207	HJ4SAMT05048	
4.74	418	HJF19X6Y8835	
3.32	872	S2549D88A24K	
1.90	707	YO683011NDX	
2.37	803	J21H08230R88	
1.89	411	TO9T874COPAP	
2.36	288	3262630028	

THE LIST OF UNDERWRITING MEMBERS OF LLOYDS IS NUMBERED 1991/

TOTAL LINE	NO. OF SYND.	FOR LPSO USE O
59.24	12	US31 676

The List of Underwriting Members of Lloyd's mentioned in the above Table shows their respective Syndicates and Shares therein and is deemed to be incorporated in and to form part of this Policy: It is available for inspection at Lloyd's Policy Signing Office by the Assured or his or their representatives and a true copy of the material parts of it certified by the General Manager of Lloyd's Policy Signing Office will be furnished to the Assured on application.

APPENDIX 4: UNDERWRITER'S TABULATION

FOR LPSO USE ONLY	SYNDICATE				LLOYD'S POLICY SIGNING OFFICE – UNDERWRITER'S TABULATION				SETTLEMENT CURRENCY	C.A. TAB. REF. MONTH/CCV/NO.	PAGE No.
XXX99R.9 999 9999	XXX				US DOLLAR CASH A/C PREMIUM				USD	XX*99*999	7

LPSO DATE	LPSO No.	BROKER No.	YEAR OF A/c	ADDITIONAL INFORMATION	CATEGORY	FIL CODE	RISK/ AUDIT	UNDERWRITER'S REFERENCE	DEBIT	CREDIT
8 10 91	52735	1234	91		A PM	5D	T	T73F88N01472		3553.57
				AMOUNT DUE FOR PAYMENT ON 14/10/91						3553.57

	M. PM/CM CR	AP/RECOV.	RP/CLAIM	NM PM/OCA	AP/RECOV.	RP/CLAIM	CUMULATIVE TOTAL FOR THIS TABULATION TYPE			
	1						CASH	0.00 *	3553.57 *	

	AV. PM.	AP/RECOV.	RP/CLAIM	TOTAL						
				1			100000.00		3553.57 **	

APPENDIX 5: BROKER'S DAILY STATEMENT

LLOYD'S POLICY SIGNING OFFICE — BROKER'S DAILY STATEMENT

US DOLLAR CASH A/C PREMIUM

FOR LPSO USE ONLY	BROKER		C.A. TAB. REF. MONTH/CCY/NO.	PAGE No.
XXX99R.9 9999 99999	1234		XX*99*999	5

LPSO DATE	LPSO No.	LATE SETT. MTHS DAYS	BROKER'S PRIME REF	BROKER'S SEC. REF	ORIGINAL CCY. NET-AMT.	EXCH RATE	CAT.	CCY/No INST. MO	INS	DEBIT	CREDIT
8 10 9	52735		DM10100000				A PM			14804.08	
					AMOUNT DUE FOR PAYMENT ON 14/10/91					14804.08	

ITEMS MARKED @ HAVE BEEN PROCESSED AT SEPARATION 1

No. OF ENTRIES THIS TAB. No.	CUMULATIVE TOTAL, FOR THIS TABULATION TYPE	BALANCE		
1	CASH 105 00.00–		14804.08 * 14804.08 **	0.00 *

APPENDIX 6: SETTLEMENT STATEMENT

L.P.S.O. CENTRAL ACCOUNTING STATEMENT

LLOYD'S
LLOYD'S OF LONDON

FOR LPSO USE ONLY

FSS30S1 0903
1

BKR 1234   U S DOLLAR

PAGE   1

FOR PAYMENT ON   14/10/91

C.A. TABULATION NO.	DEBIT	CREDIT
XX*99*999	14,804.08	
BALANCE	14,804.08	

9

GLOSSARY OF TERMS

Binding authority
An authority granted by an active underwriter to an intermediary whereby that intermediary is entitled to accept, within certain limits, insurance business on behalf of members.

Certificate of insurance
Evidence, in the form of a certificate issued in the name of the insurer, that an insurance contract exists; for example, that there is a motor insurance in force which complies with the terms of the Road Traffic Acts.

Condition
A part of a contract which must be complied with by one party or the other.

Cover note
A document issued as evidence that insurance has been granted pending the issue of a policy. (For motor insurance the cover note includes a certificate of insurance to comply with the Road Traffic Act requirements and there is usually a time limit of 15 or 30 days.)

Declaration
A statement signed by the proposer (later insured) at the foot of a proposal form, certifying the accuracy of the information given to the best of his knowledge and belief.

Endorsement
Any writing on or addition to a policy, any addition to the printed wording, which changes or varies terms of or parties to the contract.

Line slip
A line slip is an agreement between a group of underwriters and a Lloyd's broker for a specific class of insurance business, whereby certain of the underwriters may accept, on behalf of all underwriters in the group, risks introduced by the Lloyd's broker that are in accordance with the terms of the agreement.

Market agreement
An agreement between and subscribed to by all underwriters in a certain section of the Lloyd's market.

Moral hazard
The risk arising from the character and management style of the insured or his employees.

Off-slip
A broker's slip for submitting details to Lloyd's Policy Signing Office of an insurance which underwriters previously have agreed to grant.

Physical hazard
The risk associated with the subject matter of insurance.

Proposal form
An application by a proposer for insurance, on a printed form. The proposer becomes the insured when the application has been accepted and the contract brought into existence.

Prospectus
A form, which is often part of the proposal form, giving details of the cover available with particulars of extra benefits and rebates.

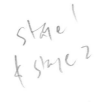

Separation
A procedure to separate the premium payment from the policy signing procedure. A slip can be signed to comply with the terms of credit requirements and the policy can be prepared and signed at a later date.

Signed line
The amount of an underwriter's line under the completed slip. This is shown in the policy in the table of definitive numbers.

Signing and accounting (S & A)
A procedure at LPSO whereby accounting procedures are conducted concurrently with the policy signing procedure.

Signing down
Where the broker overplaces a risk, the lines written by each syndicate have to be proportionally reduced so that they represent percentages of the risk actually required to be insured. This is known as short closing or reducing lines.

Signing slip
The broker's slip used for submitting details to LPSO for signing and accounting. This can be the original slip, a certified photocopy of the original slip or an initialled copy of the original slip.

Slip policy
A slip policy is a broker's slip which is made into a policy by the attachment of a special form; the purpose being to provide for those cases where the insured or the reinsured does not require a formal policy.

Syndicate reinsurance
Outgoing reinsurances placed on behalf of Lloyd's underwriters through Lloyd's brokers with other Lloyd's syndicates or insurance companies. LPSO processes reinsurance premiums and claims passing between the reinsured underwriter and his Lloyd's broker.

Table of definitive numbers
The schedule of syndicate numbers showing these syndicates' participation, which is attached to a Lloyd's policy.

War and civil war exclusion agreement
An undertaking between Lloyd's underwriters and many insurance companies generally not to accept war and civil war risks on property on land (see Waterborne Agreement below).

Waterborne Agreement
A market understanding whereby underwriters only cover marine cargo against war risks whilst they are on the vessel. This rule is relaxed only in the case of goods in a transhipping port for a short period awaiting onward carriage.

Written line
The amount or percentage written on the broker's slip by an underwriter accepting a risk to indicate the maximum liability he is prepared to accept.

9

MULTIPLE CHOICE QUESTIONS

1. What is the insured's position if his broker advises him that he is only able to place 90% of the risk?

   (a) The broker will provide cover for the unpaid 10% of the risk.
   (b) The central fund will pay 10% of all losses.
   (c) The insured is his own insurer for the unplaced 10%.
   (d) The Corporation of Lloyd's will underwrite the unplaced 10%.

2. A slip has been made out for a period of risk from 15 June to 30 September 1985 bdi. The premium is pro rata of an annual premium of £7,300.

   What is the premium for the period?

   (a) £2,160.
   (b) £2,140.
   (c) £2,120.
   (d) £2,100.

3. One class of business is such that most of it is transacted away from the Lloyd's building. To which class of business does this apply?

   (a) Marine.
   (b) Contractors' 'all risks'.
   (c) Contingency.
   (d) Motor.

4. A broker is informed of a higher value on a risk. This will result in a substantially increased line for each underwriter. The slip does not contain a leading underwriter clause. The broker takes the agreement to the leader who initials it, adding 'to be agreed three leaders only'.

   Which one of the following courses of action should the broker now take?

   (a) Ignore the leader's remark and see all underwriters before confirming agreement.
   (b) See only the next two underwriters.
   (c) See all the underwriters but feel free to advise the client of completion once he has obtained the agreement of the first three.
   (d) Re-sign the slip so that the three leaders take the extra value thereby leaving all the other lines unchanged.

5. An ambiguity in the wording of a policy will be construed against:

   (a) the broker;
   (b) the underwriter;
   (c) the insured;
   (d) LPSO.

6. A broker's cover note shows:

   (a) the agreed terms, rate, conditions and security;
   (b) only the agreed rate quoted by an underwriter;
   (c) only the list of the underwriters subscribing to the policy;
   (d) a list of insureds that the broker wishes underwriters to add to a risk.

7. What are the main sections of the cargo clauses (A), (B) and (C)?

   (a) The risks covered.
   (b) The exclusions.
   (c) The duration.
   (d) Claims.

8. Terms of credit regulations for aviation risks govern:

   (a) the maximum time allowed to pass before the underwriters receive their premium;
   (b) the periods of account settlements between broker and client;
   (c) the requirements to sign, in sterling, certain categories of currency;
   (d) only those premium entries which are signed late.

9. Which one of the following types of business is excluded from the Lloyd's central accounting scheme?

   (a) Personal accident.
   (b) Marine.
   (c) UK motor.
   (d) Short-term life.

10. Each Lloyd's syndicate has a three letter pseudonym. The pseudonym is formed from:

    (a) letters which do not have significance other than to identify the syndicate;

    (b) the initials of the underwriter;

    (c) the initials of the name with the largest share in the syndicate;

    (d) the initials of the person who has been a name in the syndicate for the longest time.

11. Separation procedure through LPSO is:

    (a) when the policy is signed before the endorsement wording is checked;

    (b) designed to separate the accounting and the signing of policies;

    (c) when the slip and premium advice note are separated from the policy after checking;

    (d) when lines written by an underwriter for a group of syndicates are separately shown for each syndicate.

12. Market agreements are intended to facilitate the processing of business and, as such, are entered into by:

    (a) Lloyd's underwriters only;

    (b) Lloyd's brokers only;

    (c) Lloyd's underwriters and insurance companies;

    (d) Lloyd's underwriters and Lloyd's brokers.

1.   Answer (c), the insured is his own insurer for the unplaced 10%.

2.   Answer (a), £2,160.

      bdi   = both days inclusive

      No. of days   = 16 days June, 31 days July,
                                 31 days August, 30 days September
                          = 108 days

      Daily premium $= \dfrac{\text{Annual premium}}{\text{No. days in year}} = \dfrac{£7,300}{365} = £20$

      Pro-rata premium = 108 days x £20   = £2,160

3.   Answer (d), motor insurance.

4.   Answer (a), ignore the leader's remark and see all the underwriters before confirming agreement.

5.   Answer (b), the underwriter.

6.   Answer (a), the agreed terms, rate, conditions and security.

7.   Answer (a), the risks covered.

8.   Answer (a), the maximum time allowed to pass before the underwriters receive their premium.

9.   Answer (c), UK motor.

10.   Answer (a), letters which do not have significance other than to identify the syndicate.

11.   Answer (b), designed to separate the accounting and the signing of policies.

12.   Answer (c), Lloyd's underwriters and insurance companies.

10

PREMIUMS AND CLAIMS PAYMENTS

A   Transfer of premiums

B   The claims handling procedure

INTRODUCTION

In this chapter we will consider the importance of the prompt and efficient transfer of premiums and payment of claims, looking at both the underwriter's and the broker's role and responsibility in these processes.

A

TRANSFER OF PREMIUMS

Any form of business involves money and, very broadly, the money of a business may be divided into two parts:

▶   money in use, whether it is income from the sale of products or services, expenditure on raw materials, wages, etc., or money invested in buildings, machinery, etc.;

▶   money kept in reserve for extraordinary expenditure, such as buying new equipment or covering trading losses.

A1 UNDERWRITER'S SOLVENCY MARGIN

For an underwriter, the money in use includes incoming premiums, outgoing claims and administrative expenditure and provision for claims yet to be met on current and expired policies. The second part of an underwriter's money, often referred to as the **solvency margin**, is the base upon which he can run the risks inherent in offering insurance protection. The bigger the solvency margin, the more risks he can run and the more business he can accept, increasing his total trade and, hopefully, profit.

However, the first call on an underwriter's money is to make provision for claims. If premiums are received

---

LEARNING OBJECTIVES

After studying this chapter, you should be able to:

▷   identify the broker's responsibilities to underwriters in the handling of premiums;

▷   discuss the importance of prompt and efficient transfer of premiums and payment of claims;

▷   illustrate the role and responsibilities of brokers in claims notification, investigation and settlement;

▷   list and discuss the role and function of Lloyd's Claims Office;

▷   demonstrate the importance to the market of prompt and efficient handling of claims.

late, he will have to make the necessary provision out of reserves, thereby reducing his solvency margin, and with it his ability to trade. Prompt payment of premium is clearly most important for this reason alone.

A2 UNDERWRITER'S INVESTMENT INCOME

As far as premiums are concerned, there is always a credit risk attached to any outstanding debt. In general, the risk increases with the length of time a debt is outstanding. However, with high interest rates, the sooner underwriters receive their premium then the longer the period they can invest it, increasing their investment income. This enables underwriters to offer more competitive rates.

In international business, fluctuations in currency exchange rates have a considerable effect on an underwriter who accounts in sterling. Whilst the effects are not necessarily adverse, it is an area outside the control and expertise of underwriters, and they much prefer to have their money in their accounting currency as soon as possible.

It is important, therefore, that there is a prompt and efficient transfer of premiums by the broker to the underwriter.

A3 THE BROKER'S ROLE

In most instances an insurance with Lloyd's under-writers must be placed by a Lloyd's broker: the insured does not have a direct contact with the underwriter. The broker is the middleman in the contract of insurance between the underwriter and the insured. (Certain business may be placed directly with Lloyd's syndicates by non-Lloyd's intermediaries or through service companies set up by managing agencies.)

The broker acts for the insured in accord with the law of agency; the insured is the principal and the broker is the agent and as such is responsible to the insured.

In consideration for the insurance, the insured is required to pay a premium to the underwriters. In the Lloyd's market this premium is transferred by the broker. The MIA 1906 provides that the Lloyd's broker is directly responsible to the Lloyd's underwriter for the payment of premiums due, whether or not he has received it from the insured. Since July 1972 payment of premium has become subject to trading terms between underwriters and the broker, whereby the broker is required to see that the premiums are transferred to the underwriters within an agreed period of credit. The late reporting system monitors brokers' performances.

Also, details of all items signed late are given to brokers to assist in their review and control of late signings. The statistics show the proportion of premiums settled late compared with the total premiums included in the scheme.

A3A Broker's lien

As a protection for the broker who has made the payment of the premium to the underwriter but has been unable to collect the premium from his client or insured, the MIA 1906 grants the broker a lien on the marine policy. A lien may be defined as a legal claim upon property until a debt on it is repaid.

Because the MIA 1906 provides that the underwriter is directly responsible to the insured for the amount which may be payable in respect of losses or in respect of returnable premiums, the Act confers upon the broker the right to retain the policy document until the insured pays him the premium.

This lien is of some value because a claim must be physically endorsed on a policy and could not be collected by the insured who does not possess the policy. In addition, the insured may require the policy to be lodged with a bank as security, or to pass to an assignee, or to send with a bill of lading to a consignee.

B

THE CLAIMS HANDLING PROCEDURE

In a real sense, the claim is the tangible result of insuring since, ultimately, most people will judge the value of the cover by the way in which a claim is handled.

The prime reason that an individual or company buys an insurance policy is that he or it identifies the possibility of pecuniary loss or liability. Should a loss or liability occur, a claim will normally be made and the insured can expect a prompt indemnification of this loss to avoid any further financial suffering, provided it is covered by insurance.

The prompt and efficient handling and collection of claims is essential, not only to reimburse the insured but also to maintain the good reputation of the underwriter.

The actual procedure for handling claims varies according to the class of business, the type of cover, the amount of the claim and whether it is a personal or commercial risk insured.

In this final section of the course book we will concentrate on the notification, submission and settlement of claims at Lloyd's. The main concern of this section will be the general procedures for claims notification, submission and settlement rather than the more detailed issues which may be specific to different types of cover.

B1 CLAIMS NOTIFICATION

The first notification of a claim can come from the insured to the Lloyd's broker or, alternatively, from the producing broker to the Lloyd's broker. (The producing broker is the original broker who obtains a proposal for business effected at Lloyd's through a Lloyd's broker.)

In the case of notification by an insured this is often given to the broker by means of a telephone call, telefax, etc., and it is essential to ensure that the personnel within the claims department should be aware of the basic details that are required from the insured (i.e. date of loss, location of loss, nature of loss, insured or address where the insured can be contacted). Notification of a claim from a ◆**producing broker**◆ to the Lloyd's broker should similarly contain the above relevant details. In certain instances a non-marine policy will contain a ◆**claims notification clause**◆. This usually designates a specific ◆**adjuster**◆ to act in respect of all claims that arise under the policy. In such cases the first

notification of a claim received by the Lloyd's broker is usually received from the adjuster nominated in the claims notification clause

It is of vital importance to ensure that the underwriters are advised of a loss with the utmost urgency so that they can ensure that their representative (i.e. the loss adjuster for non-marine risks or the Salvage Association or a consulting surveyor for marine risks) is appointed without delay. (The Salvage Association is an independent body and acts on behalf of any party who instructs it.) In many cases of direct business the insured needs to be advised continually of the progress of his claim.

The underwriter will want speedy notification of the claim and will often lay down time limits within which a claim should be intimated.

Where a potential liability claim arises, the underwriter's representative will want to be able to take statements from witnesses as soon as possible. This will also be so in respect of claims in connection with motor accidents.

In the case of theft, the underwriters will want to make sure that the claim has been intimated to the police, to allow the maximum opportunity to recover stolen property. In the case of damage to property the underwriter requires speedy notification so that action to minimise the loss may be put in hand.

In addition, some states in the USA have strict timetables governing claims handling to which insurers must adhere.

B1A Motor claims

Claims are handled by motor syndicates at their offices. On being advised of an accident or other occurrence which may give rise to a claim, the first action of a broker or the syndicate's claims department should be to issue to the insured a claims form. The insured should also be asked to pass on to the underwriters, unacknowledged, any communication which they may receive from a third party. This is because the insured may prejudice the underwriter's position if he attempts to deal with third parties himself.

Many motor underwriters use a series of claims settling agreements, whose objective is to speed up the settlement of claims and reduce claims handling expenses. Examples are the ◆**knock for knock agreement**◆ and the ◆**third party sharing agreements**◆.

B1B Life assurance claims

For life assurance claims it is important to have mechanisms in force to ensure that the insurer receives proper proof of death and that the proper legal recipients of any proceeds from a claim are identified, taking into account any will or assignments of the proceeds which may have been made for personal life policies. These procedures often involve the use of the courts.

B1C Marine claims

For hull claims, when an accident has occurred it is essential for notice (giving such details as are available) to be given promptly to underwriters through the Lloyd's brokers. The object of giving notice is to enable the underwriters to appoint a surveyor to attend the vessel and survey the damage.

An 'average' adjuster will often be employed by the insured to present the claim to underwriters. The adjuster has a duty to the insured to adjust the claim in accordance with the policy of insurance or other relevant contract, statute, rules or body of law.

Cargo claims for goods lost or found damaged on arrival at destination or before are usually advised to Lloyd's agents who arrange for surveys and who often have the power to settle the claim if the policy provides for the ◆**settlement of claims abroad (SCA)**◆.

B1D Reinsurance

There are many instances where the Lloyd's broker who places a risk is requested to arrange certain reinsurances by the underwriters that have accepted

that risk. In consequence, it naturally follows that when the Lloyd's broker advises the original underwriters of a claim he must at the same time advise the reinsurers.

B2 LLOYD'S CLAIMS OFFICE

Lloyd's Claims Office (LCO) was formed in 1992 by the merger of the three claims offices which had previously served the aviation, marine and non-marine markets:

▶ Lloyd's Aviation Claims Centre (LACC);

▶ Lloyd's Underwriters' Claims and Recoveries Office (LUCRO); and

▶ Lloyd's Underwriters' Non-marine Claims Office (LUNCO).

The office is part of the Market Services Group of the Corporation of Lloyd's but has its own board of management, comprised mainly of underwriters nominated by the market associations.

B2A Lloyd's claims schemes

The role and responsibilities of the LCO are defined in the **Lloyd's 1991 Claims Scheme** and the aviation, marine and non-marine **Past Years Claims Schemes** which apply to the 1990 year of account and earlier years. The schemes apply to all business other than motor, term life and claims administered by special committees (for example, asbestos and environmental pollution).

Claims that fall under the Lloyd's 1991 Scheme are agreed and settled by the leading underwriter on his own behalf with the LCO binding the following underwriters, provided that it agrees with the leading underwriter. For liability claims, the agreement of the first three underwriters on the slip is required before LCO can act on behalf of the following market. This can be reduced to the leading underwriter alone either through delegation of authority to LCO or by a slip provision.

The major difference between the schemes is that the Lloyd's 1991 Scheme is mandatory and therefore following underwriters are bound by the decision of the LCO, whereas under the Past Years Schemes the following underwriters may withdraw authority from LCO on individual claims and handle their proportion directly through the broker.

B2B Organisation of LCO

Lloyd's Claims Office consists of claims departments, the Recoveries Section and the General Average Section.

B2B1 Claims departments

Direct and reinsurance claims and refunds are handled within eight specialist departments:

▶ Aviation.
▶ Cargo (including cargo claims, recoveries and general average).
▶ Energy (oil and gas).
▶ Excess of loss.
▶ Liability.
▶ Marine hull.
▶ Property.
▶ Syndicate excess of loss.

These departments are involved in the handling of each claim from the first advice to final settlement. Once the broker has been informed of a casualty or potential loss, he will advise the leading underwriter and LCO (or LCO alone where the leading underwriter has delegated authority) of the details and obtain any relevant instructions. LCO will check the claim and policy details and enter the appropriate information into the claims office computer systems. Thereafter, LCO will be contacted as necessary with additional information and will give, or confirm, further instructions on a wide range of issues concerned with minimising the loss or with the presentation of the claim.

It is the LCO's responsibility to ensure that underwriters are given prompt advice of the claims and loss advices that it sees in order to enable them to assess their reserves. This is achieved via three computer systems (which are to be replaced by a common system to be implemented in 1994). The traditional card-based claims advices are being superseded by an electronic syndicate claims message which is transmitted via the London Insurance Market Network (LIMNET).

B2B2 Recoveries Section; General Average Section

The **Recoveries Section** acts for Lloyd's marine underwriters and insurance companies, both at home and abroad, in respect of claims against bailees of cargo (for example, shipowners, airlines, warehouse keepers, inland hauliers, etc.). The section works closely with the cargo claims section and is remunerated on a 'no cure, no pay' basis, i.e. fees can only be charged upon a successful recovery.

In addition, the **General Average Section** protects cargo interests in relation to general average and salvage and issues Corporation of Lloyd's 'general average guarantees'. Settlements are made under such guarantees and collections effected from the underwriters concerned. The Section is also authorised to settle general average contributions and salvage claims submitted by Lloyd's brokers.

B3 CLAIMS SUBMISSION

In submitting the claim to the underwriter, the broker should first ensure that his client has fulfilled his obligations regarding the premium payment. He will then interpret the policy conditions and present the claim to the underwriter's claims representative.

The onus is usually on the insured to prove that he has suffered a loss, by a peril which is insured by the policy; where the policy is unvalued or subject only to a limit he will be required to demonstrate the extent of the loss.

Q We have considered the responsibilities of the insured in making a claim. Can you think of some areas of responsibility applicable to the underwriter?

A The claims staff of the syndicate or the underwriter's representative in the claims office has to ensure that:

- the cover was in force at the time of the loss (or when the claim was made, under certain policies);
- the insured is that named in the policy;
- the peril is covered by the policy;
- the insured has taken responsible steps to minimise the loss;
- all conditions and warranties have been complied with;
- the quantum (amount) of the claim is correct.

The Lloyd's broker should, of course, check these facts prior to submitting the claim on the insured's behalf.

Whilst most claims fall within the policy terms, there are those where the broker has to display further skills in persuading underwriters as to the original intention of his client.

Often, a loss adjuster is appointed by underwriters to enquire into the cause of the loss and to assist in the settlement. The loss adjuster is an expert in handling claims. The adjuster is normally involved at the very early stages of a claim and will see it through to the conclusion. This will involve ensuring that all the interests of the insurer are preserved, and in checking that the cover was in force and was adequate at the time of the loss. The adjuster will also act to minimise the extent of the loss.

B4 CLAIMS SETTLEMENT

The final stage in the claims procedure is the actual monetary settlement. The claim has been notified, all parties have carried out their respective duties and all that remains is for the claim to be settled. The actual settlement, or the amount payable, depends on a number of factors, including the nature of the cover, the adequacy of the cover and the application of any conditions which limit the amount payable. For example, a fire policy will have a sum insured but this is only the limit of the liability of the underwriters and is not the amount which they have agreed to pay in the event of a claim. The eventual cost of the claim will depend on the extent of loss or damage and on the nature of the cover afforded by the policy.

When the claim is agreed, the normal process of Lloyd's central accounting system comes into play.

When underwriters agree to a ◆**special settlement**◆, this agreement will have the effect of speeding up the payment by the underwriter to the broker. It is then the undoubted responsibility of the broker to pay the insured immediately on receipt of these monies. However, with the advent of weekly claims settlement within the Lloyd's market, special settlements are rarely necessary.

The efficiency of a broker's business is most readily measured by the effectiveness of the actions of staff in dealing with claims. The basis of such efficiency must be a good recording and filing system so that papers and information are speedily extracted. The vast majority of claims are settled speedily and to the satisfaction of both the insured and underwriters.

When a dispute does arise it could revolve around a number of factors. In the main, disputes tend to be about either the liability of an insurer to pay a claim or the amount which should be paid.

Even when liability has been admitted, the determination of the amount payable in accordance with the policy terms and conditions may still be the subject of dispute. Some policies contain an arbitration clause which states that the parties must refer any disputes concerning the insurance contract to arbitration.

The Consumer Enquiries Department deals with complaints, disputes, claims problems and other matters connected with personal lines policies for UK insureds. The department also acts as an interface between the Lloyd's market and the Insurance Ombudsman for cases which have been referred to him for adjudication. Complaints must be reviewed by the department before referral to the Ombudsman.

B4A Ex gratia payments

Underwriters may make ◆**ex gratia payments**◆ on occasions. These are payments 'out of grace' (and not by right) to preserve goodwill between underwriters, the client and the broker. Such payments do not create a precedent.

Where an exclusion is a marginal one the underwriter will usually settle the claim 'wp' (without prejudice), and thus may not act in a similar fashion on a future occasion.

B5 PROMPT PAYMENT OF CLAIMS

Prompt payment of claims is simply good business practice. The right to a claim is the commodity the insured is purchasing, and an underwriter who does not pay a proven claim promptly is selling shoddy goods. In the case of domestic insurance it is largely a matter of irritation; for example, it would be infuriating to be without a car because you do not possess the money to buy a replacement whilst underwriters delay paying a claim. In business, particularly a small business, the ability to earn a living may be suspended until money is available to replace lost or damaged equipment. Prompt payment of claims is an essential element in insurance protection.

The market is selling a service and the most vital part of that service is the speedy and efficient settlement of a claim. The claims' personnel of brokers and insurers must always be able to assess priorities in order to achieve a prompt settlement. This will help the London market retain its existing business and, possibly, attract new business.

The reputation of the Lloyd's market can be damaged by slow payment of claims. The USA is particularly sensitive to slow payment of claims; powers exist in some states to compel prompt payment.

The trading conditions and standards, particularly in the USA but also worldwide, have become more complex and it is vital for the continued prosperity of the Lloyd's market that all within the Lloyd's community recognise this fact and the changes which have taken place over the last few years.

The London market, and in particular that of Lloyd's, has been synonymous with financial integrity. Thus, it must continue to provide a claims servicing capability that is beyond reproach.

There should always be prompt acknowledgement of the insured's claim, prompt investigation, prompt advice to the claimant of the result of the investigation of the claim and, if valid, prompt payment of the claim.

Everyone in the chain leading to claims settlement has a part to play in ensuring that the handling is efficient and prompt. Proper briefing from one person to another in this chain can assist in minimising delays or preventing any delay.

Lloyd's has impeccable security, thus prompt handling of claims can only enhance the position.

SUMMARY

In this chapter we have emphasised the importance of the efficient handling of both premiums and claims payments. We have recognised the importance to the market of prompt payment of valid claims, as we have seen that both underwriters and brokers benefit by efficient systems for premium transfer and for the payment of claims.

10

GLOSSARY OF TERMS

Adjuster

▶ One who investigates and assesses claims on behalf of insurers (claims adjuster or loss adjuster).

▶ One who investigates and apportions general average losses on behalf of a shipowner (average adjuster).

Claims notification clause

A clause in a policy which provides for prompt notification of claims and commonly designates a specific adjuster to receive notice and deal with the claim.

Ex gratia payment

A payment made by underwriters to maintain goodwill between underwriters, the client and the broker.

Knock for knock agreement

Agreement between insurers that in the event of accidents involving their respective policyholders neither insurer shall seek to recover from the other the insured cost of making good the damage to the vehicle insured.

Producing broker

The original broker who obtains a proposal for business effected at Lloyd's through a Lloyd's broker.

Settlement of claims abroad (SCA)

Lloyd's policies/certificates, mainly marine cargo, which provide for the adjustment of claims at destinations abroad are said to be claims payable abroad. When claims arise and are adjusted and settled by Lloyd's agents, they are handled through the SCA system controlled by the SCA office of the Agency Department. *which operates as a separate entity within LCO.*

Special settlements

A scheme under the central accounting arrangement where settlement takes place within three working days of entries being 'taken down' at LPSO.

Third party sharing agreements

Agreements between liability insurers that, when their respective policyholders are both involved in an occurrence giving rise to a third party claim, any settlement shall be shared between the insurers without apportionment of blameworthiness.

10
MULTIPLE CHOICE QUESTIONS

1. A broker handling direct marine business is liable for the premium being paid to underwriters. This custom is embodied in the relevant sections of which Act?

   (a) The Lloyd's Act 1871.
   (b) The Marine Insurance Act 1906. ☑
   (c) The Insurance Companies Act 1985.
   (d) The Lloyd's Act 1982.

2. Lloyd's policy regarding claims is to:

   (a) pay all claims submitted where the insured holds a Lloyd's policy;
   (b) pay all claims faster than in the company market;
   (c) process and settle valid claims promptly; ☑
   (d) pay all claims directly to the insured.

3. A broker's duty in the settlement of a claim ends when:

   (a) he has presented the claim to the underwriters;
   (b) he has appointed and advised a claims adjuster;
   (c) he is satisfied that the claimant has received his money; ☑
   (d) the claim has an LPSO signing number and date.

4. When a claim occurs, the balance of premium funds held by the broker against later settlement means that the broker:

   (a) can settle the claim as soon as this has been agreed by the leading syndicate;
   (b) has funds to pay the claim should it be denied by one of the participating syndicates;
   (c) can provide the claimant with an emergency fund against which to draw until the claim is settled;
   (d) can pay the claim promptly, once it has been agreed, without waiting for funds from central accounting. ☑

5. Eighteen months after a risk expires, the underwriter is shown a claim for a loss which occurred six months after the risk attached. The insured is demanding urgent settlement of his claim. The policy contains a clause requiring prompt advice of a claim. With the exception of the time delay, the claim is valid. Should the underwriter agree the claim as a 'special settlement'?

    (a) No; the late report is sufficient reason for entirely rejecting the claim. ☐
    (b) No; special settlements are not intended to be used in these circumstances. ☑
    (c) Yes; if further delay would harm the insured's business. ☐
    (d) Yes; the breach of policy condition makes this imperative. ☐

6. A broker decides to finance a marine premium payment in order to comply with terms of credit. The premium is in Italian lire. When the client pays, the broker exchanges the lire to a sterling amount considerably greater than that previously paid to underwriters. What, according to the rules, should the broker do next?

    (a) Forward the gain to a central pool from which LPSO expenses are defrayed. ☐
    (b) Keep the gain on the exchange as additional brokerage. ☑
    (c) Return the gain to the client to obtain the signed sterling equivalent. ☐
    (d) Credit the gain to the underwriters; the original signing must be amended. ☐

ANSWERS TO SELF-ASSESSMENT QUESTIONS APPEAR OVERLEAF

10

ANSWERS TO MULTIPLE CHOICE QUESTIONS

1. Answer (b), the Marine Insurance Act 1906.

2. Answer (c), to process and settle valid claims promptly.

3. Answer (c), when he is satisfied that the claimant has received his money.

4. Answer (d), the broker can pay the claim promptly, once it has been agreed, without waiting for funds from central accounting.

5. Answer (b), no; special settlements are not intended to be used in these circumstances.

6. Answer (d), credit the gain to the underwriters; the original signing must be amended.

ABBREVIATIONS

AOA	Any one accident
AOO	Any one occurrence
AO Occ.	Any one occurrence
AOP	Any one person; or any one policy
AOV	Any one vessel
AP	Additional premium
Appd	Approved
AR	'All risks'
As orig.	As original; or as original conditions
BDI	Both days inclusive
BIIBA	British Insurance and Investment Brokers' Association
Bord.	Bordereaux
CC	Civil commotions; or cancellation clause
C/N	Cover note; or credit note
Coll. Comm.	Collecting commission
Comm.	Commission
Comp.	Comprehensive
Conds	Conditions
CPA	Claims payable abroad
Ded.	Deductible
DOC	Driving other cars
e & ea	Each and every accident
e & ec	Each and every claim
e & el	Each and every loss
e & eo	Each and every occurrence
E & OE	Errors and omissions excepted
Excl.	Excluding; or exclusion
Fac.	Facultative
Fac. Oblig.	Facultative obligatory
F & AP	Fire and allied perils
fc & s	Free of capture and seizure
FDO	For declaration purposes only
FIA	Full interest admitted
FPA	Free of particular average
FSR & CC	Free of strikes, riots and civil commotions
GA	General average
HC	Held covered
H & M	Hull and machinery
IBA	Insurance broking account
IBNR	Incurred but not reported
ICC	Institute Cargo Clauses

LATF	Lloyd's American Trust Fund
LAUA	Lloyd's Aviation Underwriters' Association
LCO	Lloyd's Claims Office
LCTF	Lloyd's Canadian Trust Fund
LIBC	Lloyd's Insurance Brokers' Committee
Ll & Cos	Lloyd's and companies
LMUA	Lloyd's Motor Underwriters' Association
LPAN	London premium advice note
LPO	Lloyd's Policy Office
LPSO	Lloyd's Policy Signing Office
L/U	Leading underwriter
LUA	Lloyd's Underwriters' Association
LUAA	Lloyd's Underwriting Agents' Association
na	Net absolutely; or not applicable
NCAD	Notice of cancellation at anniversary date
NMA	Lloyd's Underwriters' Non-Marine Association
Occ.	Occurrence
OGR	Original gross rate
ONR	Original net rate
PA	Personal accident; or particular average
P & I	Protection and indemnity
PPI	Policy proof of interest
QS	Quota share
RCC & S	Riots and civil commotions and strikes
Retn	Retention
R/I	Reinsurance
RP	Return premium; or return of premium
SANR	Subject to approval no risk; or subject to acceptance no risk
TBA	To be advised; or to be agreed
TLO	Total loss only
TO	To oblige
TOC	Terms of credit
TOR	Time on risk
TOT	Terms of trade
UEP	Unearned premium
UNL	Ultimate net loss
Unltd	Unlimited
W/d -wtd	Warranted
wef	With effect from
wp	Without prejudice
W/W	Worldwide
Xs loss	Excess of loss; or excess loss

INFORMATION SHOWN ON THE TEST PAPER

The following is an example of the information with which you will be presented when you sit the Lloyd's Introductory Test. Read the following instructions carefully. An additional seven minutes will be allowed for this and a study of the answer sheet. If you do not understand an instruction, ask the invigilator to explain it to you.

INSTRUCTIONS

It is essential that candidates bring their acknowledgement of entry to the test venue as this contains their candidate number and their firm's number, both of which are required for the marking process.

General

1. This paper consists of 50 multiple choice questions, each question carrying equal marks. The time limit is 60 minutes.

2. Each question offers four possible answers, but only one is correct.

3. For each question choose what you believe, from your knowledge of practice at Lloyd's, is the correct answer.

4. You should read each question and the possible answers carefully before making your choice.

5. Record your choice on the special answer sheet provided.

6. A pocket calculator may be used for any numerical work.

7. **The test paper or pages thereof must not be removed from the room. A breach will lead to cancellation of your results.**

Notes

8. You should attempt all questions. Do not spend too long on any one question. If time permits, return to reconsider any questions which you have omitted.

9. Do not begin work on the questions until the invigilator tells you.

The answer sheet

10. Study the instructions on the answer sheet.

11. Use the pencil and, for corrections, the eraser provided.

12. Print (in pencil) your candidate's number, your firm's number (as recorded on your acknowledgement of entry form) and your name in the spaces provided at the head of the answer sheet.

13. Follow the instructions and the example shown (on the answer sheet) and encode your candidate number and your firm's number. Check these entries carefully; they are important for the computer marking process.

SELF-TEST QUESTIONS

The following 20 questions are selected from past test papers. Allow yourself 20 minutes to work through the questions in order to provide a guide as to the type of questions asked in the test. (**Note**: as already indicated, the Lloyd's Introductory Test consists of 50 questions.)

1. Which of the following facts are not material facts?

    (a)   Facts specifically relating to the subject matter of the proposed risk.
    (b)   Facts which lessen the risk.
    (c)   Facts relating to the proposer or proposers for a motor insurance policy.
    (d)   Facts relating to the refusal of other insurers to insure the proposed risk.

2. A breach of contract may arise in which one of the following ways?

    (a)   A lack of agreement to all terms of contract.
    (b)   A failure by one party to abide by contract terms.
    (c)   Discharge of the contract by mutual agreement.
    (d)   Through *consensus ad idem*.

3. Anyone who has lawful possession of the goods of another:

    (a)   always has the legal right to insure them;
    (b)   has the right to insure them only if he is liable under statute;
    (c)   has no legal right to insure them;
    (d)   has the right to insure them, but only in the insurer's name.

4. The exact replacement value of an item lost or damaged under a household policy will be paid by underwriters:

    (a)   only under a policy with an agreed value;
    (b)   under an 'all risks' indemnity policy;
    (c)   under an indemnity policy;
    (d)   if the premium paid is based on the value of the item as new.

5. A special reserve fund may only be created in accordance with conditions agreed by:

    (a)   the Corporation of Lloyd's;
    (b)   members' agents;
    (c)   the Inland Revenue;
    (d)   managing agents.

6. Which one of the following constitutes insurable interest?

   (a) The knowledge of the risk against which insurance is sought.
   (b) The potential to suffer pecuniary loss through the event against which insurance is sought.
   (c) The happening of an insured event.
   (d) The payment of a policy premium.

7. Subrogation and contribution apply to which doctrine of insurance?

   (a) Insurable interest.
   (b) Indemnity.
   (c) Proximate cause.
   (d) Utmost good faith.

8. Which of the following is deemed to be an implied warranty?

   (a) A shipowner will store all perishable cargo below deck.
   (b) A shipowner will pack all valuable cargo in tin-lined cases.
   (c) A ship is seaworthy at the outset of any voyage.
   (d) A ship will take the most direct route on any voyage.

9. The Lloyd's Act of 1982 brought into law the primary recommendation of the Fisher Working Party, which was:

   (a) that there should be divestment of ownership of managing agencies by Lloyd's brokers;
   (b) the creation of the Council of Lloyd's to administer self-regulating processes in the Lloyd's market;
   (c) that the Lloyd's Acts of 1871 and 1951 be consolidated and the Committee of Lloyd's deal exclusively with self-regulation matters in the market place;
   (d) that extensive legislation covering market procedures be drafted by Parliament over a five year period, with the assistance of the newly created Council of Lloyd's.

10. To safeguard the security of a Lloyd's policy, Lloyd's exercises control in several areas. Which one of the following is not subject to control by Lloyd's?

   (a) The loss ratio of the last closed year.
   (b) The ratio of means and deposits to allocated premium income.
   (c) The annual audit of a syndicate.
   (d) Members' funds at Lloyd's.

11. On 26 July, a broker presents to an underwriter a slip with an inception date of 1 August. The underwriter decides what percentage of the risk he wishes to accept. However, he only pencils the amount on the slip because the broker is in a hurry to get round the market.

    On 5 August the broker returns to the underwriter who puts down the line and completes his records. When is the underwriter actually on risk?

    (a) Wef 26 July.
    (b) Wef 1 August.
    (c) Wef 5 August.
    (d) He is not on risk.

12. A slip is led by an insurance company which, in turn, is followed by a Lloyd's syndicate with a line twice the size of that company's line. Under these circumstances:

    (a) the Lloyd's syndicate becomes the leader only for matters delegated to the leading underwriter by other Lloyd's underwriters;
    (b) the company underwriter is the sole leader to whom any delegation is made by other underwriters;
    (c) the insurance company becomes a following underwriter to the Lloyd's underwriter;
    (d) the role of leader is not assumed by any underwriter.

13. Proposal forms are commonly used in the Lloyd's market for which of the following classes of business?

    (a) Marine hull tankers.
    (b) Travel insurance.
    (c) A quota share treaty.
    (d) An industrial fire risk.

14. An external member of Lloyd's has to prove means of at least £250,000 in acceptable assets. However, proof of means alone does not determine the limit of premium which a member may underwrite; he must actually provide securities to the value of a fixed proportion of the proposed overall premium limit. This is required as:

    (a) a contribution to the central fund;
    (b) a premium trust fund;
    (c) a personal stop loss reinsurance policy;
    (d) funds at Lloyd's.

15. Nominated members of the Council are:

   (a) elected by ballot of working members only;
   (b) elected by ballot of external members only;
   (c) appointed by the Council and their appointment is then confirmed by the Governor of the Bank of England;
   (d) appointed by the Secretary of State, Department of Trade and Industry.

16. The Council of Lloyd's is primarily responsible to:

   (a) the Secretary of State for Trade and Industry;
   (b) no one;
   (c) the Governor of the Bank of England;
   (d) the membership of Lloyd's.

17. Who at Lloyd's is an 'annual subscriber'?

   (a) Someone who pays a subscription in order to receive all publications issued by Lloyd's.
   (b) A director of a Lloyd's broking firm, or a senior employee of a Lloyd's firm who needs to transact business in the Room.
   (c) All members of Lloyd's, since each pays an annual subscription.
   (d) Any employee of a firm connected with the Lloyd's market and who needs to gain admittance to the Room who is not a member of the Society.

18. Which of the following subject matter is **not** insurable against war risks?

   (a) Marine hulls.
   (b) Aircraft.
   (c) A person under a personal accident insurance.
   (d) Motor vehicles on land.

19. In the absence of a policy condition in his policy, when does an insured's duty of disclosure cease?

   (a) When the risk has been negotiated.
   (b) When the insured has completed a proposal form.
   (c) When the insured has received his signed policy.
   (d) When the policy period expires.

20. A standard wording is attached to a policy. Any ambiguity in the wording means that the:

   (a) contract is voidable;
   (b) wording will be construed against underwriters;
   (c) broking firm is responsible if underwriters deny liability;
   (d) contract is unenforceable.

ANSWERS TO SELF-TEST QUESTIONS APPEAR OVERLEAF

ANSWERS TO SELF-TEST QUESTIONS

1.   Answer (b), facts which lessen the risk.

2.   Answer (b), a failure by one party to abide by contract terms.

3.   Answer (a), they always have the legal right to insure the goods.

4.   Answer (d), if the premium paid is based on the value of the item as new.

5.   Answer (c), the Inland Revenue.

6.   Answer (b), the potential to suffer pecuniary loss through the event against which insurance is sought.

7.   Answer (b), indemnity.

8.   Answer (c), a ship is seaworthy at the outset of any voyage.

9.   Answer (b), the creation of the Council of Lloyd's to administer self-regulating processes in the Lloyd's market.

10. Answer (a), the loss ratio of the last closed year.

11. Answer (b), wef 1 August.

12. Answer (b), the company underwriter is the sole leader to whom any delegation is made by other underwriters.

13. Answer (b), travel insurance.

14. Answer (d), funds at Lloyd's.

15. Answer (c), appointed by the Council and their appointment is then confirmed by the Governor of the Bank of England.

16. Answer (d), the membership of Lloyd's.

17. Answer (b), a director of a Lloyd's broking firm, or a senior employee of a Lloyd's firm who needs to transact business in the Room.

18. Answer (d), motor vehicles on land.

19. Answer (a), when the risk has been negotiated.

20. Answer (b), the wording will be construed against underwriters.

LIST OF STATUTES

Assurance Companies Act 1909, 6A1A

Insurance Brokers (Regulation) Act 1977, 7B1
Insurance Companies Act 1982, 6A1A, 7D2, 7D3 7D4 & 7D5

Lloyd's Act 1871, 6A1, 6B
Lloyd's Act 1911, 6A1A, 7A2, 7A3B

Marine Insurance Act 1906, 3A, 3A1, 5B6, 10A3A

Road Traffic Act 1988, 3C, 9F1A
Road Traffic Act 1991, 3C, 9F1A

Theft Act 1968, 3B2

INDEX

INDEX

INDEX